GENDER EQUITY RIGHT FROM THE START

INSTRUCTIONAL ACTIVITIES FOR TEACHER EDUCATORS IN MATHEMATICS, SCIENCE, AND TECHNOLOGY

JO SANDERS
JANICE KOCH
JOSEPHINE URSO

LEA LAWRENCE ERLBAUM ASSOCIATES, PUBLISHERS

1997   Mahwah, New Jersey   London

This book is based on work supported in part by the National Science Foundation under Grant No. HRD-9253182. Any opinions, findings, and conclusions or recommendations expressed in this publication are those of the authors and do not necessarily reflect the views of the National Science Foundation.

The work in this project was carried out at the Graduate School and University Center of the City University of New York.

Lawrence Erlbaum Associates, Inc., Publishers
10 Industrial Avenue
Mahwah, New Jersey 07430

Library of Congress Cataloging-in-Publication Data

Sanders, Jo Shuchat.
    Gender equity right from the start / Jo Sanders, Janice Koch,
Josephine Urso.
       p.   cm.
    Includes bibliographical references.
    Contents: v. 1. Instructional activities for teacher educators in
mathematics, science, and technology -- v. 2. Sources and resources
for education students in mathematics, science, and technology.
    ISBN 0-8058-2337-9 (v. 1 : alk. paper). -- ISBN
0-8058-2887-7 (v. 2 : alk. paper)
    1. Educational equalization--United States. 2. Sex discrimination
in education--United States. 3. Mathematics--Study and teaching-
-United States. 4. Science--Study and Teaching--United States.
5. Technology--Study and teaching--United States. 6. Textbook bias-
-United States. 7. Teachers--Training of--United States. 8. Women
in mathematics--United States. 9. Women in science--United States.
10. Women in technology--United States. I. Koch, Janice, 1947-   .
II. Urso, Josephine. III. Title.
LC213.2.S25 1997
    379.2'6--dc21   97-21458
                                                        CIP

Books published by Lawrence Erlbaum Associates are printed
on acid-free paper, and their bindings are chosen
for strength and durability.

Printed in the United States of America

10 9 8 7 6 5 4 3 2 1

SUMMARY CONTENTS

COMPREHENSIVE CONTENTS

ACKNOWLEDGMENTS

Gender Equity Right From the Start is the beneficiary of many people's contributions.

We thank the funders of the Teacher Education Equity Project for their generosity and support: The National Science Foundation, IBM, Hewlett-Packard, and AT&T.

The 61 Teacher Education Equity Project participants tested, and in many cases improved on, the activities in this book with their preservice students. They have been wonderful to work with and are the heart of the project. (Contact information for all can be found in Part 4.) Those who also contributed their own teaching activities for this book to augment those of the authors are marked with an asterisk. They are:

Barbara Attivo, Wichita State University
Mike Beeth, Ohio State University
Huey Bogan, College of St. Rose
Robert Boram, Morehead State University
Rick Breault, University of Indianapolis
Cherry Brewton, Georgia Southern University
Patsy Brooks, Alverno College
Mike Cass, West Georgia College
Elisabeth Charron, Montana State University at Bozeman
Susan Chevalier, Adams State College
Frank Curriero, Jersey City State College
* Clint Erb, University of Vermont
Shirley Freed, Andrews University
Pamela Freeman, Mississippi State Univ
Donna Gee, Eastern New Mexico University
Maureen Gillette, College of St. Rose
* Mike Grote, Ohio Wesleyan University
* Karen Higgins, Oregon State University
S. Maxwell Hines, Hofstra University
Aurora Hodgden, Phillips University
Dave Johnson, Eastern Michigan University
* Karen Karp, University of Louisville
Gwen Kelly, University of Idaho
* Jody Kenny, St. Michael's College
Jerry Krockover, Purdue University
Shirley Leali, Univ. of Northern Colorado
* Barb Levin, University of North Carolina at Greensboro
Tom Lord, Indiana Univ. of Pennsylvania

* Patricia Lucido, Northwest Missouri State University
Sandy Madison, University of Wisconsin at Stevens Point
Kathi Matthew, Western Kentucky Univ.
Kathy Matthews, University of North Carolina at Greensboro
* Leah McCoy, Wake Forest University
Alice Mikovch, Western Kentucky Univ.
Rickie Miller, Boise State University
* Joyce Morris, University of Vermont
Rusty Myers, Alaska Pacific University
* Maggie Niess, Oregon State University
John Novak, Eastern Michigan University
George O'Brien, Florida International University
Ray Ostrander, Andrews University
Brenda Peters, College of St. Rose
Jenny Piazza, University of Southern Colorado
* Charlie Rathbone, University of Vermont
Joyce Saxon, Morehead State University
Dan Shepardson, Purdue University
Twyla Sherman, Wichita State University
Sheila Smith-Hobson, Lehman College
* Yee-Ping Soon, Florida International University
* Dorothy Spethmann, Dakota State Univ.
Rose Steelman, Univ. of Central Arkansas
Margaret Stempien, Indiana University of Pennsylvania

* **Korinne Tande**, Montana State University
at Northern

Marie Theobald, University of
Indianapolis

Meghan Twiest, Indiana University of
Pennsylvania

* **Martha Voyles**, Grinnell College

Frank Walton, University of Hawaii

Ken Welty, University of Wisconsin at
Stout

* **Judy Werner**, West Virginia University

* **Cathy Yeotis**, Wichita State University

Joe Zilliox, University of Hawaii

Several others also contributed activities, foremost among whom is Laura Jeffers who wrote a number of the technology activities, as well as Barbara Dannay and Marcy Ewell.

Larry Enochs and Marsha Lakes Matyas rescued the project from oblivion before it was funded when the National Science Foundation reorganized. We are immensely grateful for their tenaciousness.

The staff of the Teacher Education Equity Project have been incomparably talented and committed: Deirdre Armitage, Starla Rocco, and Dorothy Bozzone.

We are grateful to the City University of New York Graduate Center for providing a home for the project, and especially to Bert Flugman, the director of the Center for Advanced Study in Education, for his unfailing support.

The late Selma Greenberg was a pioneer in the area of gender equity in early childhood. We are indebted to her for the fine title from her book *Right from the Start: A Guide to Nonsexist Child Rearing*, published in 1978.

We are also grateful to the members of the Teacher Education Equity Project Advisory Committee:

Dennis Angle	Director, Kansas Careers, Kansas State University
Alice Artzt	Professor of Mathematics Education, Queens College
Henry Jay Becker	Professor of Education, University of California at Irvine
Marvin Druger	Past President, National Science Teachers Association, and Chair, Department of Science Teaching, Syracuse University
Elizabeth Fennema	Professor of Mathematics Education, University of Wisconsin at Madison
April Gardner	Assistant Professor of Biological Sciences, University of Northern Colorado
Peter Gerber	Director, Educational Programs, John D. & Catherine T. MacArthur Foundation
Lynn Glass	Past President, National Science Teachers Association, and Professor of Science Education, Iowa State University
Marilyn Guy	Past President, American Association of Colleges for Teacher Education, and Associate Professor of Education, Concordia College
David Imig	Chief Executive Officer, American Association of Colleges for Teacher Education
Jane Kahle	Condit Professor of Science Education, Miami University

Gavrielle Levine	Assistant Professor of Mathematics Education, Long Island University, C. W. Post Campus
Rebecca Lubetkin	Executive Director, Consortium for Educational Equity, Rutgers University
Bonnie Marks	Past President, International Society of Technology in Education, and Dirctor of Technology, Alameda County Office of Education, Hayward, California
Joann Jacullo Noto	Director of Teacher Education, Teachers College, Columbia University
Henry Olds	Senior Scientist, BBN Systems & Technologies, Cambridge, MA
Kate Scantlebury	Associate Professor of Chemistry and Biology, University of Delaware
Robert Sellar	Manager, Area External Programs, I. B. M. Corporation, New York
Charol Shakeshaft	Chair, Department of Administration and Policy Studies, School of Education, Hofstra University
Stan Silverman	Director, Educational Technology, New York Institute of Technology, Central Islip Campus
Lee Stiff	Board of Directors, National Council of Teachers of Mathematics, and Professor of Mathematics Education, North Carolina State University

Our deepest thanks are reserved for the project's evaluator Pat Campbell, for her absolute integrity, her sensitivity, her promptness and thoroughness, and her constant kindness.

> Jo Sanders, Director, Gender Equity Program
> Washington Research Institute, Seattle
> Janice Koch, Hofstra University, Hempstead, Long Island
> Josephine Urso, Community School District 15, Brooklyn, New York

PART 1

INTRODUCTION

What We Know

Decades of research support the fact that classroom environments are experienced differently by males and females. As early as nursery school, boys and girls sitting in the same classroom, with the same teacher, using the same materials, have different learning experiences. These differences persist through their pre-college education and beyond. Frequently, these experiences marginalize the girls in the areas of mathematics, science, and technology.

What we know, to generalize broadly, is that in the early elementary years girls and boys do equally well in tests and grades in mathematics, science, and technology (MST). As females progress through school and into college and graduate school, despite their frequently higher course grades, they score lower on standardized tests than males and take fewer advanced courses, which means they drop out of mathematics, science, and/or technology earlier than males.

As a consequence, large numbers of women are not qualified to enter careers in science, mathematics, technology, and related fields. The underrepresentation is easily seen in the tables in the pages later in this section. It matters because on average, technical occupations yield considerably higher salaries *for the same amount of educational preparation*. Now that a single salary can rarely support an entire family, and now that single-parent households are common, decent salaries are more important than ever. Technical occupations have relatively good career ladders. They are unusually varied: from technician to professional, and in academic, corporate, government, and non-profit settings, as well as indoors and outdoors. And they are projected to grow well over the next decade: computer engineers and scientists, for example, are expected to increase 112%. [1]

Education and employment trends concerning girls and women have been extensively studied and documented since the early 1970s. Considerable effort has been expended in reaching K-12 teachers since then with an awareness of the problem and knowledge of strategies that have been proven effective in increasing girls' participation in MST. In fact there has been measurable progress, although we are still far from equality. But gender equity progress has not for the most part reached teacher education. New teachers thus enter classrooms every year unaware that there is a problem with girls and mathematics, science, and technology, let alone how to address it. An exclusive emphasis on reaching inservice teachers makes no sense.

The reason it's important to reach preservice teachers is that gender bias in the classroom is nearly always inadvertent and, more often than you would think, below the level of consciousness. Research has shown, for example, that teachers call on boys more than girls in math, science and technology classes. Because teachers don't even realize they're doing it, they can't correct it. And although it really doesn't matter if boys are called on a little more than girls in one class period, the cumulative effect over years of schooling is to signal to children that boys' thoughts and answers are more valuable than those of girls. Indeed, it is the

---

[1] New York Times, September 3, 1995, page 9. Data from the Bureau of Labor Statistics, U.S. Dept. of Labor.

accumulation of subtle and unintended gender biases such as this that result in the severely lopsided occupational figures presented later in this section. It is not good for us as a society that women account for only 32% of chemists and 8% of engineers. *When girls and women fail to persist in mathematics, science and technology to the extent they otherwise could, this is not a women's problem. It is a human problem.*

In this book we cover gender issues in six areas:

- Mathematics, Science, and Technology as Male Domains
- Peers', Teachers', Parents', and Society's Cultural Expecations
- Biased and Inappropriate Curriculum Materials
- Classroom Interaction and Atmosphere
- Anti-Intellectualism and Attributional Style
- Testing and Assessment

We hope this book will help you acquaint your elementary and secondary preservice teachers with the gender biases to watch out for in these six areas, and how to compensate for them. It recognizes the special circumstances of courses for preservice teachers — the limited class time available, the extensive syllabus, and the field experience component. With nearly 200 activities to choose from, we are confident that you can help your students become effective teachers for girls as well as boys in all the years of their careers.

The Teacher Education Equity Project

Gender Equity Right From the Start was developed in the Teacher Education Equity Project, funded from 1993 to 1996 for $1,028,000 by the National Science Foundation, IBM, Hewlett-Packard, and AT&T. The project worked with 61 teacher educators in 40 colleges and universities in 27 states who teach methods courses in mathematics, science and technology. Its goal was to help them teach their preservice students about gender equity. A third were men, and a sixth were people of color. They taught gender equity activities to their students, shared what they learned in the project with their colleagues, and carried out a mini-grant project. The 61 teacher educators tested most and wrote some of the activities in *Gender Equity Right From the Start.*

The project clearly accomplished what it set out to do. It had a stunning multiplier effect. In only one year, the 61 teacher educators taught a total of 5,000 preservice education students about gender equity in mathematics, science, and technology. If we estimate that each new teacher will teach for 25 years and have 25 students in her/his class, these 5,000 alone will encourage 1,562,500 girls to persist in mathematics, science, and technology. Participants also taught a total of 5,000 colleagues, inservice teachers, parents, and others. And this is only *one* year's impact. The percentage of participants whose syllabi mentioned gender equity doubled (from 23% to 48%) while those whose syllabi specifically targeted gender equity increased sevenfold (4% to 27%). By a measure devised to assess pre/post teaching of gender equity, 85% of the participants changed in a more equitable direction, many quite substantially. In another pre/post measure, the percentage of participants who spontaneously mentioned the impact of gender equity issues on their lives increased from zero to 21%. Interestingly, our evaluation shows that the male participants were even more likely to make large pro-equity changes in their teaching than the female ones were.

Here are some comments by professors of education and their students about their experiences with the project.

Professors' comments

The project has changed my life, my attitude, my outlook on life itself and humanity, and my classroom behavior has improved drastically. I also discovered an interesting parallel between the gender issues and how minorities were/are treated. They are very similar. I shall continue to promote these issues and strategies, continue to monitor my own behavior, and integrate this information in all the courses I teach.

The topic of equity in general and many specific activities were easy to include in my courses. I see a good match between effective teaching and issues of equity. The project supported the goals and expectations I have for students and was not additional content to an already over-burdened curriculum.

I require students to research an aspect of gender equity that is of particular interest to them. Preservice students are amazed that data they collect on gender equity matches what the research says.

I see the importance of a calm approach. I have had several students come up to me and say, "Thank you for seeing the issues and not being angry," and "Thank you for your balance." Personally, I have a comfort level now that makes me a good change agent.

Because of the time we spent on the gender equity role playing activity the first week, the topic was brought up frequently during the semester by the students. It was as if the activity brought it to the forefront of their thinking as they worked in the schools.

I have learned that the best approach is to set students and faculty up to collect their own data. This does more than simply telling them ever could do, and has the effect of giving them responsibility and a sense of ownership of the issues.

I wanted to do something good and different in my teaching. Gender equity is the key.

Students' comments

I am startled and upset by the figures and facts I learned this semester about equity in the classroom. It is sad that women are so underrepresented in the work force, especially in math and science fields. Hopefully my knowledge of the stereotypes that occur so subtly in the classroom will keep me aware of how I interact with the students. I hope to have a classroom in which I will seek equity!

I decided to watch my Field Experience teacher one morning. She had a competition of boys against girls where she asked mini-math questions. While she was fair in that each team got a turn to answer, the questions she asked were extremely biased. The boys' questions were all about sports, while the girls' were about dresses, etc. I'm sure my teacher didn't even realize it was happening. Hopefully, studying this issue and being more aware of it will prevent me from doing it to my students in the future.

The gender equity project was one of my favorite assignments in this class.

I have learned that the main way to insure gender equity in the classroom is to make a conscious effort to do so. This means making it a point to call on girls, encourage them in math and science, and challenge them to go beyond concepts to discover new questions and answers. It means preventing yourself from showing favoritism to boys.

I feel that the knowledge I have about equality in the classroom will definitely help me to be a better teacher.

How the Book is Structured

This first volume for instructors contains general information about gender equity in mathematics, science, and technology (MST) education, teaching activities, learning assessment materials, and suggestions for action research projects to be carried out by students. **The second volume for students** contains source materials for use with various activities, as well as bibliographic and other resource listings.

In this volume, **Part I** gives you an overview of the issues and statistics on girls and women in MST education and employment for your own information and to use with your students.

PART 2, Teaching Activities, contains nearly 200 teaching activities to prepare your students to teach mathematics, science and technology equitably to girls as well as boys. They were tested (and in some cases originated) by Teacher Education Equity Project participants nationwide. In developing them, we followed several principles:

1. Whenever possible we have emphasized out-of-class and field experience activities to maximize class time for the rest of your syllabus.
2. We have designed activities not only to identify gender equity problems, but also to develop solutions for them. (We do not subscribe to the "moan and groan" school of gender equity.)
3. We have utilized constructivist and cooperative learning approaches.
4. We have provided recommendations of many resources obtainable in most college/university libraries and many handouts, to make it as easy as possible for you to teach the activities.
5. While the activities were written for science, mathematics, and technology, many can easily be adapted for use in other education courses.

The activities in Part 2 are arranged as follows:

EQUITY THEMES. Six overarching themes that have a great deal to do with female students' avoidance of MST are presented in double-line boxes.

SUBSIDIARY THEMES. Under each equity theme the details of how it is played out in classroom settings are specified and explained in single-line boxes.

ACTIVITIES. A number of activities are presented for each subsidiary theme, providing a choice of ways to familiarize your students with the problem as well as solutions. The activities are not recipes! Please feel free to adapt them as you see fit. For each activity, we specify:

- Whether it is to be carried out in class, out of class, in field work, or some combination of these three venues.
- If the activity is suitable for only one subject — mathematics, science, or technology, or suitable for only one educational level — elementary or secondary, this information is specified. When no such limitations appear, the activity is appropriate for all MST subjects and all grade levels.
- Resources needed for the activity are named. Some require student materials, which are in the "Source Materials" section of the student volume. Others are publications or programs that are referenced briefly in the activities and fully in the "Resources" section of the student volume.

The activities can be used in many ways. Here are some:

- You teach to your students the activities that fit within your specific context, even if you are able to incorporate only a few of them.
- Have individuals or groups of preservice students carry out activities themselves in a campus setting.
- Have individuals or groups of preservice students carry out activities themselves in a field classroom setting.
- Each member of the class can select (or be assigned) an activity to do. Their presentations could include written reports, visual displays, oral sharing, role plays, collages, or newsletters. Their presentations could be for you as their professor, for the class, for the "public," perhaps a college-wide event, or for local inservice faculty. Outcomes could be the preparation of units of study, lesson plans, and materials or activities for children.
- Have students select activities for group work. Varied techniques such as jigsaw could be used.

You may notice some omissions in the resources we have suggested for the activities. Decisions about what to include and exclude were based on the principle that Gender Equity Right From the Start aims at a specific point: the intersection between first, gender equity; second, teacher education; and third, mathematics, science, and/or technology education. Each of these fields has a vast literature as well as subspecialties (e.g., gender equity in children's literature, or management techniques for school science laboratories). We have omitted many excellent resources to use in conjunction with the teaching activities because they cannot be used to address all three areas of expertise. In so doing we have tried to make your identification and selection of resources more efficient.

However you choose to use the activities and however many you use, *we urge you to bring gender equity up early in the semester*. The Teacher Education Equity Project participants who tested them found that by doing so, the topic took on a life of its own for the rest of the semester. By sensitizing them to the gender issue early, they will see it in all the topics and environments they subsequently experience, thus deepening their learning greatly with no extra effort from you.

PART 3, Assessing Your Students' Gender Equity Learning, provides sample scenarios and essay questions. You will probably think of others on your own.

PART 4, Action Research Projects, presents materials to enable your students to conduct original gender equity research. As one of the participants in the Teacher Education Equity Project said, "I have learned that the best approach is to set students and faculty up to collect their own data. This does more than simply telling them ever could do, and has the effect of giving them responsibility and a sense of ownership of the issues." Long before we began using the term "constructivist," we knew that active learning was the best learning.

Many of the activities in Part 2 are appropriate for your students as action research project to carry out on their own as individual, small-group, or whole-class projects. We reference source materials located in the student volume to guide your students in their action research projects. In this volume you will find as additional possibilities for your students the action research projects carried out by Teacher Education Equity Project participants, which in some cases go beyond the scope of activities presented in Part 2. In Part 4 we also include contact information for project participants in case you would like more information on the projects they carried out. In other words, you and/or your students can carry out action research projects that are as simple or as ambitious as you choose.

Women Are Not All the Same

Throughout this book we refer to girls and women, but this is merely a convenient shorthand. There is no behavior or attitude shared by all girls or all women. Female people vary enormously in all characteristics, most definitely including learning styles.

It is also essential to remember that women come in all colors. Bulletin board displays need to show women of color as well as White women. In class discussions on gender equity, ask your students whether there are any special implications for women of color. In field assignments concerning gender equity, ask them to pay attention not only to gender in their classrooms but also to racial/ethnic groups. It does no good to advance White girls in mathematics, scienc,e and technology while ignoring the needs of girls of color.

We need in all honesty to point out that a lot of the research on gender in education has been done without disaggregating results by racial/ethnic group in addition to sex. Another limitation of existing research is that much of it is based on middle-class girls to the exclusion of working-class groups. We have been obliged to report on what is available. Perhaps your students can produce publishable-quality research that will help to right this imbalance.

Remember the Gentlemen

Many people believe that gender bias exists because men perpetuate it. Consequently, if more women were in positions of authority, influence, and power we could eradicate gender bias immediately. Right?

Wrong. There are many gender-fair men and many gender-biased women. We all began learning sexism unconsciously with the pink and blue receiving blankets we were wrapped in as newborns, and kept on learning it as children at home (think of toys for boys and toys for girls), at school, and in our communities. As we have pointed out, the men in our project did especially well. Two notable recent studies seem to support what we found by disproving the male = evil and female = virtue equations. Canes and Rosen (1995) found "no evidence that an increase in the share of women on a [science and engineering] department's faculty led to an increase in its share of female majors." [2] And a project conducted at Harvard found that women in science who had female advisers during their postdocs left science at a higher rate than those with male advisers.[3] Of course, there are many other indications that women have positive role-model effects on female students as well, which seems to mean that it doesn't matter who encourages girls to persist in MST.

This is as it should be. Gender equity is not a *female* issue but a *human* issue. Most of us, whether we are men or women, have mothers, aunts, sisters, daughters, nieces or granddaughters whose futures we care about deeply. Their lives affect ours. And considering our role as educators, this is also as it should be. We teach with our heads, hearts, and hands, not with one type or another of a reproductive system. Our shared goal, male and female educators alike, is to help the next generation achieve the most productive and satisfying lives they can — not some of them, but all of them.

Another consideration about males is that gender equity is for boys, too. It does no good to help girls build confidence and achievement in mathematics, science and technology if boys grow up believing that these are men's fields. Boys need to become men who will be secure mentors, colleagues, supervisors, and employees of women in MST. Attention to gender equity now will help that happen.

---

[2] Canes, Brandice J. and Rosen, Harvey S. (1995). "Following in her footsteps? Faculty gender composition and women's choices of college majors." *Industrial and Labor Relations Review*, vol. 48, no. 3, April issue, pages 486-504.

[3] Babco, Eleanor L., ed. (1996). "Gender disparity." *CPSTComments*. Washington, DC: Commission on Professionals in Science and Technology, January-February issue, pages 26-27.

What the Statistics Say

Several tables showing recent data on women and girls in mathematics, science, and technology education and employment are presented on the next few pages.

WOMEN IN SCIENCE, MATHEMATICS, AND TECHNOLOGY EMPLOYMENT: PARTICIPATION AND EARNINGS, 1996

Occupation	*% Female*	*Annual Earnings* *
Occupations Requiring a College or Advanced Degree		
Engineers	9	$49,300
Mathematical and computer scientists	31	45,900
Chemists	31	44,300
Biologists	37	36,300
Physicians (salaried)	31	58,900
Pharmacists	39	51,600
Registered nurses	91	$36,200
Dieticians	90	24,900
Pre-kindergarten and kindergarten teachers	98	18,800
Elementary school teachers	83	34,400
Secondary school teachers	55	36,200
Librarians	83	34,300
Social workers	68	27,200
Occupations Requiring an Associate Degree		
Electrical and electronic technicians	12	$31,700
Drafters	21	31,300
Surveying and mapping technicians	9	24,000
Biologic technicians	59	25,200
Chemical technicians	27	31,100
Computer programmers	30	40,100
Clinical lab technicians	71	$27,000
Licensed practical nurses	95	24,300
Dental assistants	98	18,800
Legal assistants	85	28,500
Occupations Requiring a High School Diploma or Apprenticeship		
Mechanics and repairers	4	$29,100
Electrical and electronic equipment repairers	12	33,500
Machinists	7	28,200
Sales workers, radio, TV, hi-fi, & appliances	21	22,000
Sales workers, apparel	75	$13,800
Secretaries	99	21,100
Hairdressers and cosmetologists	88	15,200
Bank tellers	91	16,400

* Calculated from weekly figures and rounded off to nearest $100

Source: Household Data, 1996 Annual Averages. Bureau of Labor Statistics, U.S. Department of Labor. To update statistics, contact BLS, (202) 606-6378 or check the Web at <http://stats.bls.gov>.

PERCENTAGE OF HIGH SCHOOL GRADUATES
TAKING MATHEMATICS AND SCIENCE COURSES, BY SEX, 1994

	% Boys	% Girls
MATHEMATICS		
Algebra 1	64.7	68.1
Geometry	68.3	72.4
Algebra 2	55.4	61.6
Trigonometry	16.6	17.1
Analysis/pre-calculus	16.3	18.2
Calculus	9.4	9.1

(In 1982, boys took more math than girls in all courses except algebra 1 and geometry.)

	% Boys	% Girls
SCIENCE		
Biology	92.3	94.7
Chemistry	53.2	58.7
Physics	26.9	22.0

(In 1982, boys took more science than girls in chemistry as well as physics. Then, 18.8% of boys took physics while 10.0% of girls did.)

Source: National Center for Education Statistics (1996). *The Condition of Education 1996.* Washington, D.C.: U.S. Department of Education, page 100.

----- *Compare the high school data with the postsecondary data.* -----

PERCENTAGE OF POSTSECONDARY DEGREES AWARDED TO WOMEN, 1992-1994

Field of Study	Associate	Bachelors	Masters	Doctorate
Mathematics	38	46	38	22
Biological/life sciences	59	51	55	41
Physical sciences, total	42	34	29	22
Chemistry	na	41	41	28
Physics	na	18	15	12
Computer & information scis.	51	28	26	15
Engineering	13	16	15	11

Source: National Center for Education Statistics (1996). *Digest of Education Statistics1996.* Washington, DC: U.S. Department of Education, Tables 241 and 244. Associate degree data for 1992; data for other degrees is 1994.

EDUCATION EMPLOYMENT

	Percent Women
Pre-K & kindergarten teachers (1)	98
Elementary teachers (1)	83
Secondary teachers (1)	55
Public school principals (2)	35
Superintendents (3)	7
College and university professors, full time (4)	33
College and university professors, part time (4)	45

Data Sources:

1. Bureau of Labor Statistics, U.S. Department of Labor. 1996 data.
2. National Center for Education Statistics (1996). *1996 Digest of Education Statistics*. Washington, DC: U.S. Department of Education, Table 86, 1994 data.
3. American Association of School Administrators, 1993 data.
4. National Center for Education Statistics (1996). *1996 Digest of Education Statistics*. Washington, DC: U.S. Department of Education, Table 226. 1992 data.

WOMEN EMPLOYED FULL-TIME IN COLLEGES AND UNIVERSITIES BY RACE/ETHNICITY, 1992

Field	*Total Employed Men and Women*	*% Women in Field*	*% White Women*	*% Black Women*	*% Hisp. Women*	*% Asian- Amer. Women*	*% Amer. Indian Women*
Engineering	24,431	6	3.9	0.7	0.2	1.3	—
Biological sciences	34,289	23	20.8	1.5	0.5	0.9	0.1
Physical sciences	28,313	12	10.2	0.3	0.1	0.9	—
Mathematics	25,325	25	21.6	1.0	0.6	1.2	0.4
Computer sciences	13,578	20	17.8	1.3	0.1	0.8	—
Teacher education	12,490	57	50.3	4.9	0.7	1.0	0.2

Source: National Center for Education Statistics (1996). *1996 Digest of Education Statistics*. Washington, DC: U.S. Department of Education, Table 227, 1992 data.

PART 2

TEACHING ACTIVITIES

> *OVERVIEW*
>
> *GENDER EQUITY*
> *IN MATHEMATICS, SCIENCE, AND TECHNOLOGY EDUCATION*
>
> *Gender differences in MST performance and participation are a function of contexts or situations in which these subjects are taught and learned. In order to become familiar with the dynamics of teaching them effectively and equitably to females, preservice teachers should be aware of the research defining the problem and giving recommendations on dealing with gender bias in the classroom.*

ACTIVITY 1: ASSIGNED READING   **OUT OF CLASS / IN CLASS**

1. Assign an overview of research on gender equity in MST. Many recommendations are found in Volume 2 on pages 94-96.

2. Ask students to discuss their reactions to what they have read in class, in out-of-class discussion groups, or in a written assignment, and how they think gender equity issues might influence their own teaching.

3. As a variation, ask that no more than one or two students read the same thing. Have them share what they learned with the class as a prelude to a more general discussion.

ACTIVITY 2. STUDENT RESEARCH   **OUT OF CLASS / IN CLASS**

1. At any point during the semester you can distribute the equity issue statements you will find enclosed in double or single boxes throughout this book, which we have excerpted for students in Volume II, pages 9-15. Students can choose one equity issue or "sub-issue" as a research project.

<u>**ACTIVITY 3: WHAT'S THE PROBLEM? I**</u>   **OUT OF CLASS / IN CLASS**

1. Below are 22 ways your students can begin to get a sense of why it is important to address gender equity in their classrooms; some are presented in more detail in other activities. Omit those that are not feasible in your setting, and feel free to add others.

2. Ask each student or pair or small group of students to choose one, eliminating it from the list after it has been chosen, or allow duplicate assignments. Set aside some class time for students to report to each other what they have found.

In Your College or University

- Interview or survey a representative cross-section of your peers about their career plans. Note any male/female differences.

- Obtain male/female enrollment figures for courses in computers, science, mathematics, and/or engineering, from the least to the most advanced, for the last few years.

- Obtain male/female dropout figures for the same courses in the same years.

- Obtain test scores and grades for males and females in these courses.

- Survey your peers about computers in their homes: whether there is one, how long there has been one, which room in the house it is kept, who uses it most.

- Obtain male/female figures on majors offered at your school. Compare figures for the physical sciences to those for the humanities.

- In an Arts and Sciences mathematics, science, or computer class, count the number of times male vs. female students are either called on or their called-out answers are recognized by the instructor.

- Obtain figures from the Academic Computing Lab on male/female usage and if available the amount of time males vs. females spend in the lab, or observe the lab yourself at representative times to collect this data.

In Field Placement Schools

*(Note: It will be easier for your students to collect data on children if no names
are attached but if they are simply identified as male or female.)*

- In high schools, obtain male/female enrollment figures for courses in computers, science, and/or mathematics, from the least to the most advanced, for the last few years.

- In high schools, obtain male/female dropout figures for the same courses in the same years.

- In high schools, obtain test scores and grades for males and females in these courses.

- In middle or high schools, obtain male/female figures for extracurricular activities involving math, science, or technology such as clubs, free-access computer labs, etc.

- In elementary schools, ask children to draw a scientist. Note the characteristics of the drawings and whether they differ for girls and boys.

- At all grade levels, count the number of times girls vs. boys are either called on or their called-out answers are recognized by the teacher. Compare these results in math, science, and/or computer class vs. classes such as Language Arts and Social Studies.

- At all grade levels, count the number of males vs. females pictured on classroom and/or hallway bulletin boards or showcases.

In the Community

- Analyze the gender messages in greeting cards for birth and birthdays up to age six.

- Analyze the gender messages in a toy store, with special attention to toys related to math, science or technology.

- Analyze the gender messages in children's television programs, particularly those dealing with math, science or technology.

- Keep track of all the newspaper articles you see in a given period of time concerning mathematics, science and/or technology. How many men vs. women are mentioned?

- Obtain several issues of popular magazines concerned with computers or science. Count the number of times men vs. women are pictured, are the focus of articles, and/or are the authors of articles.

- Go to a video arcade and count the number of males and females there. What are the females doing? The males?

- Go to a computer store and count the number of employees and customers who are male vs. female.

ACTIVITY 4. WHAT'S THE PROBLEM? II   **OUT OF CLASS / IN CLASS**

1. Ask students to refer to Volume II, pages 16 to 20, for:

    - EQUALS "Startling Statements"
    - "Dumber by Degrees"

2. Ask students to write a reaction to the statistics as a homework assignment.

3. Ask students to read and comment on each other's reactions and discuss how this information relates to their teaching.

4. To update "Startling Statements," contact the EQUALS program. See Resources in Volume II.

ACTIVITY 5. STARTLING STATEMENTS   IN CLASS
MATHEMATICS

1. As a variation to the preceding activity, write some of the EQUALS "Startling Statements" (see Volume II, pages 16-19) on cards and give one to each student.

2. Each student asks others for their answers or best guesses to her or his question.

3. With the various answers, students calculate the mean, median, and mode, and compare them to the right answer provided on the handout.

ACTIVITY 6. WOMEN IN THE MST WORK FORCE   IN CLASS
MATHEMATICS

1. As another variation, collect labor market statistics on women and men in various occupations. The best source is the U.S. Department of Labor, Bureau of Labor Statistics, Washington D.C. The library should have BLS publications or will be able to tell you how to obtain them. You can use the statistics on pages 9-11 in this volume, or if you prefer you can ask a student to obtain this information from the Department of Labor.

2. Select statistics that strike you as especially relevant for your field. These could be the percentage of women in selected occupations and how much women vs. men earned in them.

3. For each statistic, write a question on a card to which the statistic is the answer (e.g., "What is the percentage of ..."). Prepare enough questions so that there is one per student.

4. Distribute a card to each student, who then tapes it to the back of another student. Students therefore do not see their own questions.

5. Students circulate in the class, collecting and writing down at least five answers or guesses from classmates to the question taped on the student's back.

6. Each student calculates the mean of the estimated answers, then reads it out loud before you supply the correct answer. Students write the correct answer on their card.

7. You may want to save interesting labor force and education statistics gleaned over time from newspapers, magazines, and newsletters to use in this activity in the future. Remember to date them.

EQUITY ISSUE 1

MATHEMATICS, SCIENCE, AND TECHNOLOGY AS MALE DOMAINS

Mathematics, science and technology are perceived as male domains, from which women are thought to be absent. This erroneous belief nevertheless creates its own reality when girls and women come to feel the fields are inappropriate for them and act on it by failing to pursue MST courses beyond minimum requirements.

1A. HISTORY OF WOMEN IN MST

The apparent absence of women from many histories of achievement in MST perpetuates the myth that these fields have always been and thus are "naturally" male domains. For women to shape their futures, they must know their history. It is important to demonstrate to students that women have indeed made essential contributions.

ACTIVITY 7. RESEARCHING WOMEN IN MST I   **IN CLASS / OUT OF CLASS**

---

1. In class, ask your students to name famous women in MST history. Write the names on the chalkboard. In all likelihood, you will be able to point out that few or no women are represented. Lead a short discussion on what they think this means.

2. Assign a brief project inviting students to research the life and work of a woman in your field. You may choose to have one person research one historical figure, or have a small group of students collaborate on researching the figure.

3. Source materials on pages 21-25 in Volume II ("Famous Women Mathematians, Scientists, and Technologists") briefly summarize notable women in these fields. It can serve as the starting point for your students, or they may prefer to do their own research to find others not on our lists, in books listed in, Resources, Volume II, or others.

4. Ask students to present their findings to the class. This can be done as an oral report, written reports that are collated and distributed (for use later in their own classrooms), a role play or a skit, a Hyperstudio stack, or a Powerpoint presentation, or in any other form.

5. Lead a short discussion on students' findings. Brainstorm the reasons for women's absence from "mainstream" MST courses. Emphasize that it will be important for them to include women's accomplishments in their own classrooms, using non-textbook materials as necessary.

ACTIVITY 8. RESEARCHING WOMEN IN MST II   OUT OF CLASS
ELEMENTARY

1. Ask students to choose a notable woman in mathematics, science or technology history, and to write a one-page report on her that is suitable for children.

2. Collate students' reports and distribute a copy to each to use as teaching materials for their own classrooms.

ACTIVITY 9. TEXTBOOK ANALYSIS   OUT OF CLASS / IN CLASS

1. Have students collect recommendations from mathematics, science, engineering, and/or technology professors in the College of Arts and Sciences or Liberal Arts of major textbooks in their fields. Have them borrow at least four or five books. Alternatively, have them analyze textbooks that are used in elementary, middle school, or high school classes.

2. Individually or in small groups, students skim the books for mention of women in the contents, the text, the index, and/or the illustrations. Ask them to express their findings as a ratio of men to women mentioned or shown, or as a percentage of the total mentioned or shown.

3. Have students present and discuss their results in class. Are there any significant differences between the older and the newer books?

ACTIVITY 10. RESEARCHING WOMEN SCIENTISTS   IN CLASS / OUT OF CLASS
SCIENCE

1. In class, ask students to name famous scientists. Write the names on the chalkboard. Point out that in all likelihood few or no women are represented (except for Marie Curie). Lead a short discussion on what they think this means.

2. Assign a brief project inviting them to research and write about the life and work of five women scientists. Science majors may look for role models in their fields, such as:

   • Geology: Florence Bascom
   • Chemistry: Ellen Swallow Richards

- Astronomy: Maria Mitchell
- Biology: Barbara McClintock
- Physics: Maria Goeppert-Mayer

Resources (see Volume II for full cites):

- *Women Scientists in America: Struggles and Strategies to 1940,* by Margaret Rossiter
- *A Feeling for the Organism: The Life and Work of Barbara McClintock,* by Evelyn Fox Keller

3. Ask students to present their findings to the class and lead a short discussion on them. Brainstorm the reasons for women's absence from "mainstream" science and history textbooks. Emphasize that it will be important for them to include women's accomplishments in their own classrooms, using non-textbook materials as necessary.

ACTIVITY 11. GUEST SPEAKER   IN CLASS

1. Invite a historian of women in science to speak to your class. Contact the Association for Women in Science (AWIS) for possible names (see Volume II, Resources) or someone in your college or university who might know of local possibilities.

ACTIVITY 12. AUDIOVISUALS   IN CLASS

1. Show a videotape on the history of women in your discipline (see Volume II, Resources).

ACTIVITY 13. CLASSROOM ILLUSTRATIONS   YOUR TIME

1. Order posters on women's historical contributions in your discipline and put them up on the walls of your own classroom (see Resources, Volume II).

ACTIVITY 14. WOMEN IN HISTORY RECEPTION   IN CLASS

1. Invite students to select a woman scientist, mathematician, or technologist to research.

2. At the last class of the semester, hold a reception for students who attend dressed as the person they chose to research.

1B. LACK OF WOMEN INVENTORS IN CURRICULUM

The lack of women inventors in texts and other standard curriculum materials gives the erroneous impression that women did not invent anything. Learning about women inventors dispels this myth.

ACTIVITY 15. ELLEN SWALLOW RICHARDS   OUT OF CLASS

SCIENCE

1. Ask your students to research Ellen Swallow Richards, who invented a method for testing the purity of water in Massachusetts at the turn of the 20th century, was the first female professor at M.I.T., and was the originator of the science of home economics.

2. Ask them to write a brief description of the Boston Women's Laboratory that she founded in the late 1800s and what processes and products were explored in her lab.

ACTIVITY 16. WOMEN OF INVENTION   OUT OF CLASS

SCIENCE, TECHNOLOGY

1. Ask your students to read about the invention of the cotton gin, credited to Eli Whitney. Then ask them to explore Catherine Greene's patent for the cotton gin, now recognized by the U.S. Patent Office. Ask: Why do the textbooks still credit Eli Whitney with this invention?

2. Order the *Women of Invention* Poster Pack from the National Women's History Project (see Resources, Volume II). Distribute posters to groups of students and have them teach each other about these women. Were there any surprises in the packet? Which one(s)? Why?

3. Ask students to consult some books in the library on inventors and their inventions. How much of a presence do women have in these books? Stress the importance of challenging females to be creators of new ideas and projects. Use this information to challenge your students to integrate women of invention into their teaching.

ACTIVITY 17. WHERE ARE THE WOMEN INVENTORS?   IN CLASS / OUT OF CLASS

SCIENCE, TECHNOLOGY

1. In a class discussion, ask students to brainstorm a list of inventions (the cotton gin, the printing press, the sticky note, and the telephone are some obvious ones that may come up, as well as the computer). Who made these inventions? How many of the inventors are women?

2. Refer students to "Women Inventors" (Volume II, page 26) and ask students to review it. Are there any surprises?

3. Each student chooses a woman inventor from the list or from a book by Anne L. Macdonald, *Feminine Ingenuity* (see Volume II, Resources), and researches her invention as an oral report, written reports that are collated and distributed (of use later in their own classrooms), as a role play or a skit, as a Hyperstudio stack, or a Powerpoint presentation, or in any other form.

4. Results of their research are shared in class.

1C. INVISIBILITY OF CONTEMPORARY ROLE MODELS

The invisibility of women as contemporary scientists, mathematicians, and technologists generates and reinforces girls' belief that these fields are male activities which do not welcome women's participation. Without role models, it is hard for girls to envision themselves as potential specialists in these fields, and many opt out of continued study.

ACTIVITY 18. GUEST SPEAKER   **IN CLASS**

1. Invite one or more women working as a scientist, engineer, mathematician, or computer specialist to speak with your class. Options:

   - Invite someone you know.
   - Ask your students to suggest possibilities they know of.
   - Ask the local chapter of the Association for Women in Science (AWIS), the Society of Women Engineers (SWE), or the Association of Women in Mathematics (AWM) to recommend a speaker, or ask women in these departments at your university (see Volume II, page 107 for a list of organizations for women in MST).
   - Invite a senior or a graduate student on the recommendation of the department chair or faculty.

2. Ask the woman to talk about her career path and prospects, and describe what it is like to be a woman in the field. Have students prepare questions for the visitor in advance.

ACTIVITY 19. WHOM DO YOU SEE?   **IN CLASS**
                                                      TECHNOLOGY

1. In a class discussion, ask students whom they ordinarily see working in computer and electronics stores: men or women? Who are the faculty members of the computer science department at your college or university, and who staffs the academic computing center? Whom do they see using technology in the media (newspaper and television news reports, television dramas, movies, literature such as science fiction, etc.)? If they never noticed before, have them go out and look.

2. Discuss students' conclusions and their significance.

ACTIVITY 20. INTERVIEW A WORKING WOMAN   IN CLASS / OUT OF CLASS

1. Ask your students to collaborate on the preparation of five to ten interview questions to ask of a woman earning her living as a mathematician, scientist, engineer, or technologist. They should be the questions to which the students are most interested in learning the women's answers: background, training, career path, salaries in the field (in general, not in particular), work environment, men in their field, work/family issues, or anything else. Of particular interest might be memories of their school teachers' influence on their careers, positive or negative.

2. Students interview one or two such women individually or in pairs. For identification suggestions, see Activity 18 (Guest Speaker).

3. Students can discuss their findings in out-of-class or in-class discussion groups, as oral reports, written reports that are collated and distributed (of use later in their own classrooms), as a role play or a skit, as a Hyperstudio stack, or a Powerpoint presentation, or in any other form.

ACTIVITY 21. SHADOW A WORKING WOMAN   OUT OF CLASS

1. Instead of interviews, you can ask your students to shadow a woman earning her living as a mathematician, scientist, engineer, or technologist. This means spending half a day or more with the woman accompanying her as she works.

2. Students can process their findings in the same ways as in the preceding activities.

3. How does what these women *do* relate to how we *teach* mathematics, science, or technology?

ACTIVITY 22. CREATE A WALL DISPLAY   OUT OF CLASS / IN CLASS

1. Ask your students to search newspapers, popular magazines, professional publications, and/or the Internet for articles and photographs of women in your discipline.

2. With this material ask them to create a bulletin board in the classroom that shows at least as many women as men. Emphasize that this is an activity they can do with their own students.

ACTIVITY 23. ANALYZE PUBLICATIONS   **OUT OF CLASS**

1.   Ask students to search newspapers and professional publications for people currently working in your discipline. You can assign a specific publication to each student or let them choose their own; if it's long, specify a limit of 50 or 100 pages.

2.   Ask them to count the following:

   • The number of women and men pictured in illustrations, by race as well.
   • The number of women and men mentioned in articles.
   • The number of women and men listed as authors of articles.

3.   Students can discuss the ratios they found in out-of-class discussion groups, they can present them graphically, they can write them in a short report, or you can discuss them in class.   They can also send their findings to the publishers in a letter to the editor. This is an activity they can do with their own students.

ACTIVITY 24. AUDIOVISUAL   **IN CLASS**

1.   Show a videotape on women currently in mathematics, science and/or technology careers (see Resources, Volume II, page 103).

ACTIVITY 25. ELECTRONIC MENTORING   **OUT OF CLASS**

1.   Surf the Web for current information on women in mathematics, science and technology. Suggest that students participate, even if only as "lurkers," in listservs and discussion groups consisting of women in these disciplines (see Volume II, Resources, for sources current as of 1996).

1D. REINFORCEMENT OF MALE STEREOTYPES IN MEDIA

When media — movies, television, radio, newspapers, magazines, books, computer software, and others — show the vast majority of mathematicians, scientists, and technologists as male, girls (and boys) understand this as descriptive of reality. It is a small step to prescriptive: It is "normal" and "natural" for these people to be male. This becomes a self-fulfilling prophecy.

ACTIVITY 26. PUBLIC LIBRARY   OUT OF CLASS

1. Ask students to ask a librarian at a public library to help them identify ten fiction and/or non-fiction books about mathematicians, scientists, or technologists without specifying gender. How many of the ten turn out to be male? Does it make a difference if the books are for children or for adults?

ACTIVITY 27. TELEVISION ANALYSIS   OUT OF CLASS

1. Divide television-watching time assignments among your students, an hour or two per person. Be sure to include some prime time, news, and Saturday morning children's programming. Ask them to record the number of times they see a mathematician, scientist, or technologist shown, the gender of the person, and whether the person is presented as attractive or odd.

ACTIVITY 28. MAGAZINE ANALYSIS   OUT OF CLASS

1. Ask students to analyze recent issues of popular magazines in the library for gender bias. Examples are *Omni, Discover, PC Computing, Popular Mechanics*, and *Popular Science*. They can:

    • Count illustrations of men and women who have a connection with mathematics, science, or technology, by race as well as sex. What are they doing? How are they portrayed?
    • Count male and female authors of articles, as indicated by first names.
    • Where appropriate, count male and female subjects of articles.

2. If the issues have been purchased, students can make collages to illustrate their conclusions.

ACTIVITY 29. PROFESSIONAL ASSOCIATION MATERIALS   OUT OF CLASS / IN CLASS

1. Ask for a volunteer to send away for career materials from professional associations in your discipline.

2. Have this person report to the rest of the class what she or he found in terms of illustrations and language: Are they balanced or primarily male? What are the implications?

ACTIVITY 30. MOVIE CRITIQUE I   OUT OF CLASS / IN CLASS

1. Ask students to name old and current movies, especially science fiction films, that feature mathematicians, scientists, and/or technologists. (Some possibilities are Jurassic Park, Star Trek movies, 2001: A Space Odyssey, Back to the Future movies, and Free Willie.) To augment their list, they can canvass their friends or make a field trip to a video store.

2. In pairs or small groups, have students choose one movie to rent and critique concerning the role of women shown in the movie. They should consider:

    -   Who does what work?
    -   What are the relationships among men and women?
    -   How are people dressed?
    -   Are the MST people portrayed positively or negatively? Does this vary according to their sex?
    -   Does the date of the movie correlate with how women are portrayed?

3. Back in class, ask students to report on what they found. What are the implications?

ACTIVITY 31. MOVIE CRITIQUE II   OUT OF CLASS / IN CLASS

1. Ask students to make a videotape of clips of movies such as those in the preceding activity. They can identify the movies as above, then identify short segments they find especially revealing of sex roles. Your university may be able to help them with facilities to transfer the segments onto a single videotape.

2. Show the videotape in class, and discuss its meaning.

ACTIVITY 32. CHILDREN'S LITERATURE   **OUT OF CLASS**
ELEMENTARY MATHEMATICS

1. Students create an annotated bibliography of children's literature that is used to teach your discipline. In mathematics, for example, students can include:

   - *Caps for Sale* (Slobodkina, 1989)
   - *The Door Bell Rang* (Hutchins, 1986)
   - *Frog and Toad Are Friends* (Lobel, 1970)
   - *Counting on Frank* (Clement, 1991)
   - *Crocodile's Coat* (Irons, 1992)

2. Have them note the way females and males are portrayed in the books in terms of gender bias.

3. The bibliography can be entered in a data base that can be revised and expanded by your students and ultimately used in their classrooms.

ACTIVITY 33. WOMEN IN MST AND THE MEDIA   **OUT OF CLASS**
SCIENCE

1. Ask your students to research the media coverage of women who won the Nobel Prize in chemistry, medicine, or physics (refer students to "Women Nobel Prize Winners" on page 27, Volume II), or any women named for science achievement in the press.

2. Invite them to analyze this coverage in terms of the role of women in our culture. Recommended reading is the chapter on "The Mystique of Science in the Press" in *Selling Science* by Dorothy Nelkin (see Resources, Volume II).

3   Ask them to write about how the press presented the women's personal attributes and their work. How does the press portray women in mathematics, science, and technology? To what extent is the portrayal of these women in opposition to the cultural expectations of women in general?

1E. THE CULTURE OF MST FAVORS MEN

The culture — the mores, environments, ways of doing things, systems of reward and punishment — of mathematics, science, and technology is one that reflects its male history and therefore has many traditionally male features: competition over cooperation, hierarchy, aggressiveness, long hours that exclude family time, and others. Women and girls may feel uncomfortable and unwelcome in this culture, which can however be altered with the presence of a sufficient number of women and men willing to consider new ways.

ACTIVITY 34. READING   **OUT OF CLASS / IN CLASS**

1. Assign any of the following articles on women and the culture of science, mathematics and technology to the students in your class (see Resources, Volume II, for full cites).

    • Angier, Natalie (1991). "Women Swell Ranks of Science, But Remain Invisible at the Top"

    • Fryer, Bronwyn (1994). "Sex and the Superhighway"

    • Harding, Sandra (1986). *The Science Question in Feminism*

    • Keller, Evelyn Fox (1990).   "Long Live the Differences Between Men and Women Scientists"

    • Lewis, Ellen (1993). "Hers: Making a Difference"

    • Matyas, Marsha Lakes (1985).   "Obstacles and Constraints on Women in Science: Preparation and Participation in the Scientific Community"

    • Quindlen, Anna (1993). "Birthday Girl"

    • Raffalli, Mary (1994). "Why So Few Women Physicists?"

    • Rosser, Sue V. (1990). "What I Learned from the Bag Lady Scientist and the Nobel Laureate James Watson"

    • Spertus, Ellen (1991). "Why Are There So Few Female Computer Scientists?"

2. Ask preservice teachers to reflect on the traditional attributes of scientists, mathematicians, and technology specialists in western culture and list some of these commonly held traits for a class discussion.

1F. ISOLATION OF GIRLS AND WOMEN IN MST

While sociologists of science and related fields assert that the meritocracy works, stories from the field by women indicate that isolation within the community of male scientists is prevalent. Females entering MST fields need to develop strategies for dealing with this marginalization.

ACTIVITY 35. WOMEN SCIENTISTS ON THE MARGINS   OUT OF CLASS

SCIENCE

1. Assign one of the following articles to a third of the preservice teachers (full cites in Volume II):

    •   Keller, Evelyn Fox (1985). "A World of Difference" in *Gender and Science*, an essay about Barbara McClintock

    •   Sayre, Anne (1975). *Rosalind Franklin and DNA*

    •   Hubbard, Ruth (1976). "Rosalind Franklin and DNA"

2. Ask preservice teachers to write a brief reaction paper on their essay, with reference to the ways in which these two world-class scientists dealt with the gender isolation of their scientific work.

3. Ask preservice teachers to share what they learned with peers who read the other essays.

ACTIVITY 36. EXPLORING GIRLS' SELF-IMAGE   IN CLASS

TECHNOLOGY

1. Ask students to consider the following passage:

For the women, involvement with technology has been a generally empowering experience. They describe feelings of increased competence and capability as a result of their chosen work. However, these women also experience a number of conflicts related to their involvement with technology. For more than half the women in this sample, the major conflict has to do with their experience of themselves as women in arenas that remain largely the province of men. They often feel themselves to be different, to be outside the mainstream, to be the objects of curiosity and scrutiny both within and outside their professional networks. As a result, many women described work situations in which they feel compelled to overcompensate — to be better than their male colleagues.

"Women and Technology: A New Basis for Understanding" (News from the Center for Children and Technology, October 1991)

2.   Ask them to consider any similar conflicts they may have had in relation to their use of technology.

3.   Lead the class in a discussion of how these feelings can influence one's involvement in technology, and how they might address the issue of girls' and women's conflicted self-image in their teaching.

EQUITY ISSUE 2:

PEERS', TEACHERS', PARENTS', AND SOCIETY'S CULTURAL EXPECTATIONS

The notion that males excel in mathematics, science and technology is one of many beliefs and cultural influences that are passed down from generation to generation. Teachers, parents, and others transmit signals to children about who can succeed in MST. The dynamic is all the more powerful in that they themselves may not realize they hold these beliefs and act on them. The subtle and unintended messages can create the belief among girls that they cannot be successful in these fields. When children perceive this attitude in adults, children reflect and reinforce it through their interactions with their peers. This cultural expectation becomes a self-fulfilling prophecy — a cycle that continues to discourage women's participation in MST.

2A. BIASED BELIEFS ABOUT WHO SUCCEEDS IN MST

When teachers, parents, and peers believe that males will perform better in mathematics, science, and technology than females, many girls internalize this belief and behave accordingly. When parents' biased beliefs lead them to feel that these fields are inappropriate choices for a girl, they can discourage their daughters from persisting in them, either actively or by failing to encourage them. It is important to identify gender-based beliefs that have no basis in reality in order to dispel them.

ACTIVITY 37. DRAW AN MST PERSON I   IN CLASS

1. Ask your students to draw the common perception of a scientist, mathematician, or technologist. If they are already doing field work, ask them instead to draw the picture as they think the children in their school would draw it. Tape the drawings to the wall.

2. How frequent are these stereotypes? Wild hair, glasses, lab coat, fizzing beaker or test tube, male, old, no other people in scene, facial hair or zits, pocket protector, arcane formulas on chalkboard, and so forth.

3. Ask students what these stereotypes suggest to girls. Emphasize the asocial nature of the stereotyped specialist as being in opposition to the typical socialization of females, and also frequently in opposition to the social nature of the work many of these specialists do in reality.

4. Note that the scientist stereotype, by depicting scientists as weird and asocial is limiting for many boys as well.

ACTIVITY 38. DRAW AN MST PERSON II   **FIELD / IN CLASS**

1. Ask students to have the children in their field placement schools draw a scientist, mathematician, or technologist.

2. Have students analyze the drawings for five factors:

   - Affect: What are the person's feelings?
   - Setting: Home, school, workplace, elsewhere?
   - Tasks: What is the person doing in the drawing?
   - Details: What else about the person or the surroundings is shown, and why?
   - Size: Is the person large or small in relation to the MST object(s), and what might this mean?

3. In class ask students to tape the most representative drawings to the wall and to explain their findings.

ACTIVITY 39. REMEMBERING   **IN CLASS**

1. Ask students to form pairs and talk about what they remember from their early school years about what they felt others — especially parents and teachers — expected of them as a girl or a boy in terms of mathematics, science, and/or technology achievement. Were these expectations the same as their brothers or sisters had? Knowing what they now know, what would they as teachers do to break the hold of some of the limiting expectations they remember?

2. Ask students to share what they remembered with the rest of the class.

ACTIVITY 40. WHAT WOULD LIFE BE LIKE AS THE OPPOSITE SEX? I   **OUT OF CLASS / IN CLASS**

1. Assign the following topic for homework, to be answered in writing. (Refer students to "Life as a Member of the Opposite Sex," page 28 in Volume II.)

Imagine waking up tomorrow morning as a person of the opposite sex. Consider the following questions:

1. *How would your behavior change? Would you be more active or less? More outspoken or less?*
2. *How would your clothing change? Would you be more comfortable or less?*
3. *Would other people treat you differently? If so, in what ways?*
4. *Would your students treat you differently? How?*
5. *Would you be more or less involved with mathematics, science, and technology? In what ways?*

2. In a class discussion, ask students to share their conclusions with one another. Do any patterns emerge?

3. Refer students to "My Daddy Might Have Loved Me," page 29 in Volume II, which contains the answers of children to this question. Ask students what the implications are.

ACTIVITY 41. WHAT WOULD LIFE BE LIKE AS THE OPPOSITE SEX? II   FIELD / OUT OF CLASS

1. Ask students to carry out the preceding activity with children in their field placement classrooms by having children write their answers, making sure the children identify themselves as boys or girls. Students can have children write answers to any of the five questions in Activity 40, or simply respond to the main question only.

2. Ask them to analyze the results for a homework assignment. What conclusions do they draw? This is also excellent as an action research project.

3. You may choose to warn your students that children's responses may be similar to those in "My Daddy Might Have Loved Me" (Volume II, page 29) — in other words, quite disturbing. It is not unusual for some boys to respond that if they were girls they would kill themselves.

ACTIVITY 42. EXPECTATIONS   IN CLASS

1. Ask students to close their eyes and imagine a classroom, then to write five adjectives that describe a "typical" boy and a "typical" girl of an age they will be teaching.

2. Compile a list of their adjectives on the chalkboard under the headings "Negative" and "Positive" such as:

<table>
<tr><td>NEGATIVE CHARACTERISTICS</td><td>POSITIVE CHARACTERISTICS</td></tr>
<tr><td>Aggressive</td><td>Assertive</td></tr>
<tr><td>Talkative</td><td>Inquisitive</td></tr>
</table>

3. Comparing their adjectives, discuss how similar behaviors can be perceived as different.

4. Compare expectations and perceptions of male and female behavior, and how these can affect the teaching and learning of mathematics, science, and technology.

ACTIVITY 43. SURVEYING THE STUDENTS   **FIELD / IN CLASS**

1. Invite your students to develop a questionnaire for the children in their field placement classes about attitudes toward MST as a subject and in terms of careers.

2. As an alternative, refer students to "Sample Attitude Survey Questions," (Volume II, pages 31-33). As another alternative, students can ask children to list careers that men are interested in and careers that women are interested in. These lists reflect students' beliefs about gender and careers.

3. Ask students to discuss their conclusions in class. If you would like them to pool their results, they all need to use the same method. Students could publish their findings in the university newspaper and/or, with your guidance, in a professional journal.

ACTIVITY 44. SURVEYING THE TEACHERS   **FIELD**

1. Ask your students to ask the teachers of science, mathematics, and/or technology in their field placement schools who their top students were over the last three years. In fact, they should ask the question two ways: who got the best grades, and who was the most talented? The answers may differ.

2. In analyzing their results, what did students find out about gender and achievement in MST? Again, consider publication of the results on campus or in a professional journal.

ACTIVITY 45. SELF-REFLECTION I   **OUT OF CLASS**

ELEMENTARY

1. Ask your students to write an essay describing the attributes they believe successful scientists, mathematicians, or technologists have. Ask them whether they think of these attributes as masculine, feminine, or gender-neutral.

2. Invite students to reflect on these attributes in terms of where they do or do not fit in, and to think about whether the attributes are genuinely or only stereotypically sex-typed.

ACTIVITY 46. SELF-REFLECTION II   **OUT OF CLASS / IN CLASS**

SECONDARY

1. Ask students to write about how they became interested in majoring in MST. Who influenced them as they grew up?

2. Invite them to share their stories and identify barriers, if any, to their choice of a major.

2B. CHOICE OF MATERIALS BY TEACHERS AND PARENTS REINFORCE SEX STEREOTYPES AND PRODUCE NEGATIVE ASSOCIATIONS

The choice of materials such as toys, books, and clothing reinforces cultural expectations of female behavior. Girls who are not exposed to toys and materials that encourage scientific, mathematical or technological thinking and activities are less likely to develop an interest in these subjects, thus reinforcing the belief that they are not for girls. Similarly, when girls are exposed to materials negatively portraying women in these areas, they are discouraged from maintaining their interest in them.

ACTIVITY 47. READING ASSIGNMENT   OUT OF CLASS

1. Ask students to read Chapter 6, "Sexism in Textbooks," on pages 73-91 in *Female-Friendly Science* by Sue Rosser (see Resources, Volume II).

2. Ask them to write a brief essay on how they envision applying what they have read to their own teaching.

ACTIVITY 48. EXPLORING A TOY STORE   OUT OF CLASS

1. Assign students in small groups to explore the pink and purple aisles of a large toy store. Ask them to list the toys and games that are found in these aisles. Is the packaging designed to appeal to girls or boys? What types of behaviors do these items foster?

2. Ask students to look for chemistry and erector sets and for toys that incorporate electronics. What aisles are they found in? What kind of packaging do they have? In what ways do they encourage boys and discourage girls?

ACTIVITY 49. EXPLORING THE MAGAZINES   OUT OF CLASS
                                                                            SECONDARY

1. Ask students to explore the images and articles in recent issues of teen magazines such as *Seventeen Magazine, YM,* and *Sassy.* Are there any female scientists, mathematicians, or technologists presented there?

2. If students could summarize the message about being female that each magazine gives to young women, how might they sum it up?

ACTIVITY 50. ACTION RESEARCH IN SCHOOLS   FIELD / OUT OF CLASS

1. Have each student select two girls in the same class in their field placement schools: a successful MST student and an unsuccessful MST student. Students should be comparable in academic ability with the exception of their MST achievement.

2. In class, discuss and decide which research components your students would like to include:

    *   Observations of the two students during a lesson
    *   Interviews with them about their attitudes about and achievement in MST
    *   Interviews with their teachers about the girls' performance in class
    *   Interviews with their parents about beliefs concerning their daughters' MST ability
    *   Observation of the girls' choices of toys, hobbies, play patterns, etc., as appropriate
    *   Review of the girls' MST test history: standardized tests and teacher-made tests

3. Have students observe the girls during two or more classes and conduct the selected research components.

4. Students describe in writing what circumstances, materials, behaviors and attitudes seemed to influence the successful student that are not present for the unsuccessful student.

ACTIVITY 51. BIASED MATERIALS   OUT OF CLASS

1. Ask students to examine toy catalogs, store advertisements, and multimedia displays for items that support MST learning. They should analyze illustrations and written descriptions for gender allusions or content.

2   They can collect pictures and by cutting and pasting, and can create their own advertisements that model equity in MST and can be used in their own classrooms for bulletin boards and activity center displays.

ACTIVITY 52. INTERVIEW STUDENTS   **FIELD**
                                                                            TECHNOLOGY

1. Ask students to interview children in their field placement classes about home computers. Questions can include the following:

    - Is there a computer at your house or at a friend's house? If so:
    - What room is it in?
    - Who uses it most in the family?
    - What kinds of software do you use there?
    - Who chooses the software?

2. Ask students to write up their interview findings, noting differences, if any, between boys' answers and girls'.

2C. CULTURAL AND PARENTAL INFLUENCES CAN WORK AGAINST MST FOR GIRLS.

In some cultures, parents discourage females from pursuing fields in science, mathematics, or technology. This can create problems for teachers who encourage female students, and conflicts for the girls who find these subjects interesting and exciting. Preservice teachers need to be sensitive to parents' attitudes, beliefs and cultural issues about who succeeds in MST.

ACTIVITY 53. RESEARCH JIGSAW   OUT OF CLASS / IN CLASS

1. Discuss the following question with your students:

    Should cultural styles influence learning and teaching?

2. Assign articles related to culture and learning styles to groups of students. Articles can include:

- Guild, Pat (1994). "The Culture/Learning Style Connection" in *Educational Leadership*
- Shade, Barbara J. and New, Clara A. (1993). "Cultural Influences on Learning: Teaching Implications" in *Multicultural Education: Issues and Perspectives* (See Resources, Volume II)

3. Have students process this material using the jigsaw method. A) For these two articles, assign half the class to read each article. B) Have the two groups discuss the article they have read. C) Re-divide the class into pairs consisting of "representatives" of each of the two readings. D). In each pair, students describe to each other the articles they read.

4. Call the class together to discuss what they learned from this activity.

ACTIVITY 54. CULTURE AND BARBIE   IN CLASS / OUT OF CLASS

1. Have students measure a Barbie doll and/or a Ken doll, and project real-life measurements using ratio and proportion.

2. Discuss the implications of these role models for boys and girls.

3. Ask students to read:

- Quindlen, Anna (1994). "Barbie at 35" in the New York Times

4. Ask students to discuss how culture — defined as knowledge, concepts, values, beliefs, and symbols shared by a group through systems of communication — can influence women as exemplified by the Barbie doll.

ACTIVITY 55. VIGNETTE: MARIA'S BROTHER BOBBY   IN CLASS

                                                                        SECONDARY

1. Ask students to discuss the following vignette. It is available for students on page 34 in Volume II. If you teach mathematics, you can revise the vignette by substituting an advanced mathematics course.

   Maria's brother Bobby was first in his class in advanced placement chemistry. Maria, who is two years younger, demonstrates excellent science skills as well. The science department chair is concerned, however, when Maria does not choose any advanced placement or honors science courses as a high school senior, even though she is well qualified.

   When asked, Maria explains that she's interested in the AP course but her parents don't think she should take it. The chair asks the parents to attend a conference. Maria's parents explain to the chairperson that they do not think it is necessary for Maria to take advanced placement science. They fear that it will be too difficult for her and lower her grade point average.

   If you were the department chairperson, what would you do to help change Maria's parents' attitudes toward her participation in the chemistry course?

ACTIVITY 56. FAMILY MATH, SCIENCE, OR TOOLS & TECHNOLOGY   OUT OF CLASS

Note: Family Math, Family Science, and Family Tools & Technology programs are often sponsored by schools and/or districts to encourage parents to join their children in doing MST activities. For information, contact EQUALS, the Consortium for Educational Equity at Rutgers University, and/or Northwest EQUALS (see Volume II).

1. Ask your students to find out which local school districts sponsor any of these events for parents and their children.

2. Ask them to attend and write a description of the event.

3. Who has come to the event? How many girls and boys, what ages and grade levels, which parents? Observe the attitudes and behaviors of girls and their parents.

ACTIVITY 57. PARENT INVOLVEMENT PROGRAMS   OUT OF CLASS

1. Have your students contact local education departments or recognized national parent programs such as Family Math (see Resources, Volume II), to learn about programs that are offered to parents to encourage the participation of girls and minorities in mathematics, science, and technology.

2. They can create a data base of these programs and their locations for future reference.

ACTIVITY 58. PARENT WORKSHOPS   FIELD

1. Have your students contact local schools for the time and location of parent workshops in mathematics, science, or technology, and offer to assist with or at least to observe one or more workshops. Ask them to pay particular attention to the attitudes of parents of girls.

2. Ask them to write a summary of their observations.

ACTIVITY 59. CULTURAL ISSUES   OUT OF CLASS / IN CLASS

1. Ask your students to research cultures that are locally significant to understand the contributions of those cultures to the development of mathematics, science, or technology. In **mathematics**, for example, Asian cultures invented the calendar and the concept of place values in the number system. Egyptians gave us the Eye of Horos hieroglyphic and Egyptian multiplication (doubling and halving factors). In **science**, Native American contributions to ecology are well documented, especially crop rotation, soil preservation, and the importance of preserving and sustaining natural resources. A good resource for this is *Keepers of Life* by Michael Caduto and Joseph Bruchac (see Volume II, Resources).

2. During the research process, they should note the traditional behavior expected of women in those cultures and if MST and women are thought to be compatible.

3. Students discuss what they have learned in class.

2D. LACK OF AWARENESS OF GENDER BIAS

Gender biased beliefs are both taught and expressed by the subtle and unintentional behaviors of parents, teachers, and peers. Pre-service teachers who are gender biased, most definitely including young women, will pass this bias on to their students the same way it was passed to them. Preservice teachers need to identify their own bias and investigate ways of counteracting biased behavior.

ACTIVITY 60. TESTING ONESELF   IN CLASS / FIELD

Note: Activities in Equity Issue 4 may also be useful to test oneself.

1. When you have a student teach a mini-lesson to the rest of the class, ask the non-teaching students to observe the "teacher" for any of a variety of biased classroom behaviors. These can include:

    *   Language — e.g., "guys, man, or mankind" to refer to female people
    *   Eye contact — making eye contact more with males than females
    *   Calling on students — calling on males more than females
    *   Body position — standing near a cluster of males rather than females

2. As an alternative, ask students' cooperating teachers to observe them for biased behavior in field placements.

3. In a class discussion, process students' findings. Make it clear to students that biased behaviors are unintentional, that all of us share them to some extent, and that therefore no one is blaming anyone. But we can "cure" ourselves of these behaviors by becoming consciously aware of them and teaching differently.

ACTIVITY 61. AWARENESS PORTFOLIO   OUT OF CLASS / IN CLASS

1. Ask your students to consider their own science, mathematics, or technology autobiographies by writing a personal statement on gender beliefs in relation to teaching and learning. In it, ask them to reflect on their memories of how girls and boys were treated by others in MST classes, how they themselves felt as a girl or a boy in terms of learning MST, and what their beliefs about girls and MST are now.

2. Students begin a gender portfolio consisting of:

    *   Research articles on gender and MST and summaries of their reactions
    *   Popular coverage of gender equity and MST as found in newspapers, magazines, movies, television, and so on.

- A written assignment on what they have learned: a self-evaluation based on the portfolio.

3. Hold a class discussion of what they have learned about themselves.

ACTIVITY 62. TEACHER EXPECTATIONS   **OUT OF CLASS**

                                                                        MATHEMATICS

1. Assign "Standard 3: Knowing Students as Learners of Mathematics" from NCTM's *Professional Standards for Teaching Mathematics*, pages 144-147.

2. Have preservice teachers react to Standard 3 by preparing a written response to the following question:

   How can I, as an elementary/secondary school teacher, ensure full participation of my female students as well as my male students in mathematics?

3. This response can become part of the preservice teachers' Awareness Portfolio (see the preceding activity) or can be kept in a journal.

ACTIVITY 63. SURVEY TEACHERS AND ADMINISTRATORS   **FIELD / IN CLASS**

1. Invite your students to ask administrators and professors/teachers at both your college or university and at their field placement schools the following question:

   Is there a gender equity problem with mathematics, science, or technology in schools?

   A. No.
   B. Yes, but not at this school.
   C. Yes, in general and at this school.

   Please explain your answer.

2. In a class discussion, ask students what the most common response was. Which answers were the most interesting, and which were the most articulate? Was there a difference by respondent category?

ACTIVITY 64. COUNTING GIRLS   FIELD / OUT OF CLASS

SECONDARY

1. Ask your students to count the number of girls at their field placement schools in optional and advanced MST classes as well as extra-curricular MST-related activities. The latter might include clubs, contests and competitions, special events, free-time computer or lab use, etc.

2. Ask them to write up their findings. Is there a substantial difference in the number of boys and girls in these classes and activities?

3. If they find a large gap in girls' and boys' participation, ask them to talk with teachers and administrators at the school. Are they aware of the imbalance? Are they concerned? Are there any efforts under way to address it?

ACTIVITY 64. WHAT DOES THE LAW SAY?   OUT OF CLASS / IN CLASS

1. Ask students to read "Federal Anti-Discrimination Laws Pertaining to Schools" on pages 35-38 of Volume II for summaries of relevant legislation. Your reference librarian will know how to direct students to copies of the complete legislation. If for some reason this is not possible, have students call their local congressperson's office and request copies.

2. At a minimum, all students should become thoroughly familiar with Title IX of the Education Amendments of 1972 as amended by the Civil Rights Restoration Act of 1988, which is essential for every educator to know. It prohibits discrimination on the basis of sex against any student or employee in all programs of a school district receiving federal financial assistance. In addition, ask each student to research one other piece of legislation.

3. In a class discussion, ask students to describe for each other the legislation they have researched. Now that they are familiar with Title IX and at least some legislation relating to schools, can they think of incidents or conditions either from their own earlier experience or in what they observe in field placement schools that might be against the law? What would appropriate responses be?

2E. LACK OF TECHNIQUES TO COUNTERACT BIAS

Once teachers become aware of the problem of gender bias, what are they supposed to do about it? When when they don't know, gender imbalances continue unchecked. Becoming aware of the issues is an important first step, but without knowledge of what to do awareness is futile.   The next step in breaking the cycle of bias is to learn about proven techniques used in early intervention or outreach programs that counteract bias and inequity, and strategies that work to address biased cultural expectations for females in mathematics.

ACTIVITY 66. PARENTAL ATTITUDES   **OUT OF CLASS / IN CLASS**

                                                                                              TECHNOLOGY

1. Explain to your students that parents often don't realize that their home computer may be dominated by the male members of the household. By tracking who uses it and for how long, inequities can be recognized and then addressed.

2. Have students ask three families to track how computers are used in their home for one week by having a "sign-up" sheet at the computer. Each time someone uses the computer, they record who is using it (man, woman, boy, girl), for how long, and what they use it for. Also have the families note the room in which the computer is located.

3. Ask students to compile their findings in writing and note the following:

- Who used the computer most?
- What was it used for? Which applications were the most popular? Any differences in terms of adults vs. children? Males vs. females?
- Who played games? Which ones? Any differences in terms of adults vs. children? Males vs. females?
- Is there any relationship between where the computers are located and who uses them?
- What conclusions can be drawn from these findings?

4. Hold a discussion in class about the recommendations your students can make to these families and the families of the children in their classes in years to come concerning avoiding bias in home computer use.

ACTIVITY 67. MEET THE MST WOMEN   **IN CLASS**

1. Invite women scientists, mathematicians, or technologists from your college or university to speak to your students.

2. Ask your students to generate a list of questions for these women that would help to clarify the possibilities of the life of a woman in these fields.

3. Ask students to reflect on any barriers and struggles these women may have encountered.

4. Ask them to develop a list of strategies to overcome some of these identified obstacles, and to revise their "interview" questions to a form suitable for the age range of the children they will be teaching for the purpose of classroom visits in future years.

ACTIVITY 68. ANALYZING BELIEFS ABOUT GIRLS' LEARNING   IN CLASS

1. Refer students to "Questions for Teachers Who Want to Enhance Student Learning," Volume II, page 39. These questions are about mathematics, but they are equally valid for science and technology.

2. Ask your students to work in small groups to research and discuss the issues as they relate to their own teaching, and share their reactions and responses.

3. Groups identify what issues they feel are most important and present them as a panel discussion in class.

ACTIVITY 69. EXPLORING INTERVENTION PROGRAMS   OUT OF CLASS

1. Provide your students with a list of intervention programs for girls in science that have proven successful in counteracting media and cultural bias. They include:
   - Operation SMART
   - Eureka Teen Achievement Program
   - Brookhaven Women in Science
   - National SEED Project (Seeking Educational Equity and Diversity)
   - Mathematics, Engineering, and Science Achievement (MESA)
   - Saturday Science Academy
   - SummerMath
   - Females Achieving Mathematics Equity (FAME)
   - EQUALS/Family Math
   - GESA
   - Family Science
   - Family Tools and Technology

They are listed in Volume II, Resources. Most are also described in *Breaking the Barriers: Helping Female and Minority Students Succeed in Mathematics and Science* by Clewell, Anderson and Thorpe (see Resources for full cite).

2. Ask students to research at least three programs. What attributes do these programs have in common? Who is the intended audience? What strategies do these programs promote to encourage females? How are these programs evaluated? Which of their strategies may be institutionalized in mathematics, science, and technology classes?

3. If possible, students should visit a program and/or interview the program director. Ask them to prepare a report detailing:

   - What equity issues does the program address?
   - Who is the intended audience for the program: parents, teacher, students?
   - What techniques are used to counteract biased beliefs?
   - How does the program measure its effectiveness?

ACTIVITY 70. VIGNETTE: AS A HIGH SCHOOL TEACHER   **IN CLASS OR OUT OF CLASS**

SECONDARY

1. Ask students to read the following vignette from page 40, Volume II. (If you teach Science Methods or Technology Methods, change the course names from math courses.)

   As a high school teacher you regularly teach Basic Mathematics and Advanced Mathematics. One of your best students in the Basic course is Aisha, and you have been encouraging her to sign up for Advanced Mathematics next year.

   Today she stays after class to talk to you. "I've been thinking about what you said about taking Advanced next year," she says. "I've talked to a lot of my friends about it. They all say that only boys take Advanced, or maybe boys and a dorky girl. I went to the math club after school. There were only boys there and they acted like jerks. I didn't want to be there so I never went back. I'd hate being the only girl in the class, so I'm not going to take it."

   What, as Aisha's teacher, would you say to her? What would you do?

2. Have students discuss this situation in class, including how they felt as "the only one" at some point in their lives, or ask them to write their responses as a homework assignment.

ACTIVITY 71. TECHNOLOGY VIGNETTES   OUT OF CLASS / IN CLASS
TECHNOLOGY

1.   Ask students to read the following vignettes from page 41, Volume II.

A.   There is an after-school computer club at your school, and you've been encouraging your female students to join. Several have taken you up on your suggestion, but have dropped out rather quickly. When you ask them why, they tell you that the other club members were mostly boys, that the girls weren't very much interested in what the boys were doing, and in any case were not invited to participate. In addition, the room was plastered with images of males wielding technology, including posters from male-oriented movies and sorcerers and wizards from a variety of battle-oriented computer games.

B.   You have two computers in your elementary classroom that are available for students to use as they like. Invariably the boys beat the girls to the machines and then monopolize them for long periods of time, telling the girls that computers are for boys. The girls find other activities that interest them.

C.   Several of your female students who have shown an interest in computers and technology have told you that their families are discouraging them from continuing their studies. Their families, they say, are concerned that technology is not "women's work," and that they will not be happy or accepted if they pursue careers in the field.

D.   You have encouraged several of your female students to enroll in the advanced programming course at your high school. One of them told you recently that her student advisor counseled her against it, saying that the class was very technical and that she would find it difficult to keep up with the other students (currently all boys).

2.   In class or out of class, have preservice teachers share and discuss their responses.

EQUITY ISSUE 3

BIASED AND INAPPROPRIATE CURRICULUM MATERIALS

Curriculum materials that are male-biased in language, content, and/or illustrations reinforce for females the idea that mathematics, science and technology are male domains. The situation is further complicated by materials that focus on abstractions and procedure-based learning, which only reinforces beliefs that these subjects are impersonal and irrelevant to real life. This is especially problematic for females, who by using biased curriculum materials will see MST as unrelated to their daily life experiences in and out of school and will not be able to envision themselves using these skills in their adult lives as citizens or workers.

3A. CURRICULUM MATERIALS SHOW A PREDOMINANCE OF MALES

When curriculum and classroom materials present notions of male presence and female absence or male activity and female passivity, girls are reinforced in a belief that MST is a male activity. It is important to identify any male bias in curriculum materials and compensate for it.

ACTIVITY 72. READING ASSIGNMENT   **OUT OF CLASS / IN CLASS**

---

1. Ask students to read "Teaching the Majority" by Sue Rosser on pages 42-43 in Volume II, which concerns the phases of women's absence and presence in the curriculum from women's total absence to reconstructed curriculum that includes everyone. Another excellent resource, too long to reproduce here, is Peggy McIntosh's " Interactive Phases of Curricular and Personal Re-Vision: A Feminist Perspective." (See Resources, Volume II, for full cite.)

2. Hold a discussion in class on the implications of Dr. Rosser's (and Dr. McIntosh's) curriculum theories.

ACTIVITY 73. WOMEN IN CURRICULUM MATERIALS   **IN CLASS**

1. Refer students to "The Forms of Bias in Instructional Materials," Volume II, page 44.

2. In class, have students examine a variety of older as well as more recent curriculum materials and note the types of bias that are found.

3. Present a chart to be completed by the students in pairs or groups:

    Type of Bias   *Examples From Curriculum Materials*

    Invisibility
    Imbalance
    Stereotyping
    Unreality
    Fragmentation
    Linguistic bias
    Cosmetic bias

4. Have students share their findings, particulary about whether they vary according to publication dates, and discuss how they would counteract each type of bias as the teacher of an elementary or secondary class.

ACTIVITY 74. VIGNETTE: YOU ARE ABOUT TO START...   **IN CLASS**

1. Ask students to read the following vignette, found on page 45, Volume II. (If you teach Science Methods or Technology Methods, change the course names from math courses.)

    You are about to start your student teaching in Ms. Smith's classroom. You have spent considerable time learning about gender equity in mathematics education in your methods course, and how biased materials can discourage girls from persisting in mathematics.

    When you enter the classroom, you can't help but notice the bulletin boards are decorated with pictures of famous male mathematicians. The textbook the children are using contains many gender-stereotyped themes such as girls calculating recipe quantities and boys calculating sports averages. The supplementary print and audiovisual materials used with the class are also gender biased.

    You are disturbed to notice that the girls seem to participate less in class discussion. They seem to sit back and let the boys answer questions, and seem less interested overall in the class than the boys.

    What would you do about this situation? Why?

2. Ask pre-service teachers in small groups to discuss the case study and brainstorm how they would handle the situation.

ACTIVITY 75. SURVEYING TEACHERS AND COORDINATORS   FIELD / IN CLASS

1. Ask students to speak with people in the field placement school to which they have been assigned who would be knowledgeable about selection of curriculum materials. This might be their cooperating teachers, the department chairperson or a principal or vice-principal. They should explain that they are contributing to a class survey on the extent to which teachers or other school personnel consider the portrayal of girls and women when ordering textbooks or supplementary reading materials. Have them ask: *To what extent is gender equity a criterion for the adoption of curriculum materials?*

2. Conduct a class survey and record the results. How many respondents consider female roles when purchasing instructional materials?

3. Discuss the responses students received. They might consider giving the survey results to the cooperating teachers and school administrators who participated as a way to influence future purchasing decisions.

ACTIVITY 76. CLASSROOM MATERIALS IN SCHOOL   FIELD

1. Ask students to analyze posters, bulletin boards, and other materials visible in the classrooms and corridors of their field placement schools. How many women and how many men are pictured? How are they described? What are these people doing? Do any of the images or words reveal sex-role stereotypes?

2. Have them write a brief report on their findings.

3. Ask them to design a bulletin board display that highlights female contributions to mathematics, science, and/or technology and put it up in their field placement classroom.

ACTIVITY 77. CLASSROOM MATERIALS IN YOUR UNIVERSITY   OUT OF CLASS

1. Ask students to analyze posters, bulletin boards, and other materials visible in the classrooms and corridors of your college or university. How many women and how many men are pictured? How are they described? What are these people doing? Do any of the images or words reveal sex-role

stereotypes?   Do results differ for buildings that house departments of physical sciences, mathematics, and technology on the one hand and departments of fine arts and humanities on the other?

2.   Have them write a brief report on their findings.

ACTIVITY 78. RESTORING WOMEN'S PRESENCE I   OUT OF CLASS

1.   After having identified the extent of the relative absence of women in curriculum materials by means of any of the preceding activities, have students brainstorm ways to counteract it. Where will they find resources to put women back into the curriculum?

2.   Have students divide the following resources among them and send for enough catalogs and resource lists from each source to provide one to each student (addresses in Resources, Volume II).

   • National Women's History Project
   • WEEA Publishing Center
   • Organization for Equal Education of the Sexes, Inc.

3.   You can also have them contact the National Science Teachers Association (1840 Wilson Blvd., Arlington VA 22201, 703/243-7100), the International Society of Technology in Education (1787 Agate St., Eugene OR 97403, 541/346-2400), the National Council of Teachers of Mathematics (1906 Association Drive, Reston VA 22091, 703/620-9840), and/or your State Education Department (you'll know this address) to request any materials they have on girls and women in sufficient quantities for the students.

4.   Distribute copies to each student of the materials they collect. Emphasize the need to use these materials in their own classrooms.

ACTIVITY 79. RESTORING WOMEN'S PRESENCE II   OUT OF CLASS

1.   Ask students to create an ongoing collection of materials showing balanced portrayals of both sexes in MST. The collection can contain:

   • Newspaper and magazine pictures and articles
   • Names and publishers or samples of good curriculum materials
   • Names and publishers of posters or actual posters

2.   Students can share their collections with each other for future reference.

3B. WOMEN ARE SHOWN IN TRADITIONAL ROLES

Males and females are often assigned traditional roles in the materials that students are exposed to, reinforcing the idea that MST are male fields and that women are expected to be helpers, at best. Similarly biased representations in print and software materials as well often go unnoticed, especially because they are so familiar, and the biases are communicated to children. Reviewing materials with an eye to such bias helps preservice teachers develop awareness of the issues and be more discriminating in their selection of materials.

ACTIVITY 80. EXPLORING CHILDREN'S MAGAZINES   OUT OF CLASS / IN CLASS

1. Invite your students to analyze children's magazines that focus on or include math, science and/or technology for the roles in which females are portrayed. Ask them to count the number of females depicted in the magazine they select. Descibe the female images. What are they doing? In what roles are they engaged? Are these different from how males are shown?

2. Ask students to write a paper describing what they examined and their findings.

3. Conduct a class discussion evaluating these results.

ACTIVITY 81. SURVEY VIDEO GAMES   OUT OF CLASS / IN CLASS
     TECHNOLOGY

1. Ask students to play several video games in the local arcade, pizza shop, or college student union, noting the roles of females in the games (if any). Are there any female heroines? If they are not heroines, what are women's relationships to the heroes? How much violence is involved? How is the player rewarded for doing well? How would the average pre-teen or teenage girl react to these characteristics?

2. Ask them to observe the other customers at the video games. How many females do they see? Is there a sex difference in who is watching and who is playing?

3. Invite students to share their observations in a brief class discussion.

ACTIVITY 82. MATH IN GENDER-TRADITIONAL CAREERS   IN CLASS / OUT OF CLASS

MATHEMATICS

1. Ask students to list careers that are considered traditionally female, such as nurse, teacher, childcare giver, and so on.

2. Have them shadow or interview women in traditional roles, observing or asking about when and how they use mathematics.

3. Hold a discussion about the kinds of mathematics students find that women in traditional roles actually do, and the importance of mathematics to that career.

**ACTIVITY 83.   GENDER-TRADITIONAL WORK
        AS A MATH RESOURCE**   IN CLASS / OUT OF CLASS

MATHEMATICS

1. Ask students to bring in samples of directions for activities that are considered traditional women's work, such as cooking, knitting, and so on, or visit a museum and look at traditional work from different cultures.

2. List the mathematics topics needed to follow these directions. For examples, ask students to read "Real-Life Mathematics" (Volume II, pages 46-47).

3. Ask students how they can use this information in their teaching.

ACTIVITY 84. NON-TRADITIONAL ROLES   IN CLASS / OUT OF CLASS

MATHEMATICS

1. Ask students to list careers and roles that are considered non-traditional for females.

2. In groups or pairs, have them develop a list of questions that can be used to interview women in non-traditional roles, concerning what mathematics was studied, the people who influenced their studies, attitudes toward mathematics, and so on.

3. Students interview women in non-traditional roles or careers.

4. Students share with the class what they believe to be the major factors that encouraged these women to pursue non-traditional roles or careers in mathematics.

3C. MATERIALS DO NOT REFLECT GIRLS' INTERESTS

Many times girls lose interest in mathematics, science, and technology because they find the content based on interests frequently held by males and not females. While it is important to avoid reaching out to girls *exclusively* through the traditionally limited areas that they have been encouraged to engage in, such as cooking and sewing, it is important that preservice teachers find ways to involve girls in MST through content that truly interests them.

ACTIVITY 85.   IDENTIFYING STUDENT INTERESTS   OUT OF CLASS

1. Prepare the following assignment sheet from the NCTM Standards for students to complete as a homework assignment. (It is reprinted on page 48 in Volume II.)

    The National Council of Teachers of Mathematics' Professional Teaching Standards states the following:

    "Teachers also need to understand the importance of context as it relates to students' interest and experiences. Instruction should incorporate real-world contexts and children's experiences, and, when possible, should use children's language, viewpoints, and culture..."

    In the space below, list what you would do as an elementary/secondary teacher to identify your female students' interests and experiences.

2. Have preservice teachers exchange their assignment sheets for review and comments.

ACTIVITY 86. CHILDREN'S OPINIONS OF VIOLENT SOFTWARE   FIELD

TECHNOLOGY

1. Ask your students to interview children in their field placement classes about their opinion of violent software. What kind of software to they consider violent? How do they feel about it? How do their friends feel about it? Why?

2. Have students compare the responses of boys and girls.

ACTIVITY 87. SOFTWARE STORE   OUT OF CLASS / IN CLASS

TECHNOLOGY

1. Ask students to visit a software store and examine the recreational software, CD-ROMs, and multimedia packages displayed for children. What themes are common? Do they appeal more to boys or girls? Why?

2. Hold a class discussion of the implications of their findings for the home lives of the children they will have in their classrooms, and how what they learn from recreational software can influence their attitudes and performance in school.

ACTIVITY 88. PROBLEM CHOICES   IN CLASS / FIELD

1. Have students work in pairs or groups to select three problems in mathematics or science that are similar in length, readability, content, and difficulty, that focus on: a) sports, b) cooking, and c) pets.

2. Ask students to administer these items to a class, allowing children to choose two of the three problems they are presented with.

3. Students analyze which problems the children selected by gender and ethnicity to determine if the problem's context influenced their choice.

4. Discuss how the context of a problem can encourage or discourage interest or participation in mathematics, science, or technology.

ACTIVITY 89. HOW WOMEN AND GIRLS RELATE
          TO TECHNOLOGY   IN CLASS / OUT OF CLASS

TECHNOLOGY

1. Ask students to read "Gender and distance learning" by Cornelia Brunner (1991). See Resources, Volume II, for a full cite.

2. Lead a class discussion on how they might incorporate this information about the ways women and girls are interested in technology in their teaching.

3. Ask them to brainstorm technology learning activities that would be likely to appeal to girls. Can they come up with activities that are likely to appeal to both girls *and* boys?

ACTIVITY 90. INTEREST INVENTORY   IN CLASS / FIELD

MATHEMATICS

1. In groups or pairs, ask your students to develop an interest inventory for elementary or secondary school children. The inventory can include:

    • Extra-curricular activities such as hobbies, sports, games, and so on.
    • In-school activities such as favorite subject, clubs, and so on.

2. Ask students to administer the inventory to children in their field placement class.

3. Have students design mathematical tasks based on the results of the inventory, reflecting students' interests. They should include mathematics content, skills, and applications that are appropriate to each activity.

4. Students share the tasks with their cooperating teachers for review.

ACTIVITY 91. KITCHEN INGREDIENTS   IN CLASS

ELEMENTARY SCIENCE

1. Ask your students to name some familiar kitchen ingredients that are suitable for science lessons. For example, it is possible to conduct an experiment with cooking oil and karo syrup, or with baking soda and vinegar.

2. Ask them if they can think of a way to demonstrate states of matter that should be familiar to girls (and boys). One way surely is making scrambled eggs. The beaten eggs and milk are liquid, the cooked eggs are solid, and the gas escapes as steam as the eggs are cooked.

ACTIVITY 92. DISSECTING CHICKENS AND FROGS   FIELD

SECONDARY SCIENCE

1. If your students are doing their field work when biology students are beginning frog dissections, before the dissection is scheduled they can bring in several whole chickens from the supermarket. They should ask the biology students to remove the fat and skin from the chickens and to separate the legs and thighs from the body of the chicken. This activity generally involves girls more than boys and prepares students well for the Rana pipiens experience.

2. As an alternative, have some students carry out the chicken procedure while others launch into the frog dissection directly. Do they observe any difference in girls' attitudes and behaviors during dissection between the two groups? What about the boys' attitudes and behaviors?

ACTIVITY 93. CHILDREN'S VIEW OF TECHNOLOGY I <u>**FIELD**</u>

ELEMENTARY TECHNOLOGY

1. Ask students to interview several children in their field placements regarding technology and gender. Some questions they might ask are:

    *   Does the computer have a name?
    *   Is the computer a he or a she? How do you know?
    *   Are characters in your favorite software boys or girls? How do you know?
    *   If you are familiar with Logo, does the turtle have a name? Is it male or female?
    *   Can you think of any software that has girls in it? Any with boys?
    *   Do you have a computer at home? If yes, who uses it most? For what? Who buys the software?
    *   Do you think you will use a computer for work when you grow up? For what?
    *   Are girls or boys better at computers, or doesn't it make a difference?

2. Ask them to write a brief paper or create posters to represent their interview findings. Did they find a difference between boys' responses and girls'?

ACTIVITY 94. CHILDREN'S VIEW OF TECHNOLOGY II <u>**FIELD**</u>

TECHNOLOGY

1. Have your students observe boys' and girls' behavior using computers, and the cooperating teachers' interactions with computers and the children using them. Are there any gender differences in who uses the computer, when, for what purposes, how, and for how long?

2. Ask them to write a brief paper on their findings.

3D. MATERIALS DO NOT REFLECT THE REAL-LIFE RELEVANCE OF MST

Making the connections of MST concepts to everyday life, such as a practical use for a scientific discovery or a mathematical algorithm, or understanding everyday phenomena, fosters the interest and particpation of girls much more than materials that do not make connections and deal with depersonalized, abstract concepts.

ACTIVITY 95. READING ASSIGNMENT   OUT OF CLASS

1. Ask students to read Chapter 5, "Toward Inclusionary Methods," pages 55-72 in *Female-Friendly Science* by Sue Rosser (see Resources, Volume II, for full cite).

2. Ask them to write a brief essay on how they envision applying this material to their teaching.

**ACTIVITY 96.   EXPLORING THE RESEARCH
                 ON MAKING CONNECTIONS**   OUT OF CLASS / IN CLASS
                                                                         SCIENCE

1. Have students read "Breaking the Mold: Celebrating Individual Differences in the Science Classroom" by Janice Koch and and Susan Blunck, on the importance of connecting students' lives to their science experiences (see Volume II, Resources).

2. Discuss the reading in class by having each student select the passage she/he found most surprising, important, or interesting and arrive at class prepared to read and discuss that passage.

ACTIVITY 97. CONTEMPORARY ISSUES IN MST   OUT OF CLASS / IN CLASS

1. Have students use daily newspapers and weekly news magazines to identify contemporary science, mathematics and technology issues. One possibility is Tuesday's "Science Times" section of the New York Times; call 1-800-NYTIMES to order.

2. Invite them to discuss these articles in terms of experimental design and outcomes. Who is doing the research? Who is funding it? Ask them to come prepared to class to discuss a science issue of current importance that they are particularly interested in. Why did they choose this article? In what way does it interest them? Take a class survey exploring contemporary issues that are most pressing for the group.

3. Ask students to consider the implications of this discussion for making MST issues relevant to girls' lives.

ACTIVITY 98. DAY-TO-DAY MATHEMATICS   OUT OF CLASS / FIELD

MATHEMATICS

1. Ask students to develop a list of day-to-day activities that involve mathematics, such as:

   • Time schedules
   • Personal and family budgeting
   • Modifying a recipe to make more or less than originally intended
   • Comparing the cost of driving to that of taking public transportation (secondary)
   • Determining how much salary a person would need to cover expenses

2. Have preservice teachers write a mathematics task that allows female students to construct meaning by building on and extending knowledge practiced in real life.

3. Have students design spreadsheets based on the activities, and carry out one or more spreadsheet ideas with students in their field placement schools.

**ACTIVITY 99. LIFE WITHOUT MATHEMATICS,
            SCIENCE, OR TECHNOLOGY**   OUT OF CLASS / FIELD

1. Have students keep a record for one day of every time they hear, read, see, use, or think about something that involves mathematics, science, or technology. Are they surprised at the number of incidents they record? What would life be like without mathematics, science, or technology? What does this imply for the everyday nature of the subject?

2. Have them write three problems or class activities based on these incidents and carry them out in their field placement classes.

ACTIVITY 100. RESOURCE LIST   OUT OF CLASS

MATHEMATICS

1. Students visit libraries, bookstores, teacher centers, and so on. and select at least ten mathematics publications such as student textbooks, activity books, work books, and problem-solving materials.

2. They review the materials and classify them according to type of resource: for teachers, students, or parents.

3. They examine each publication for real-life applications of mathematics.

4. Using a data base, they enter a brief review of the material by publisher, author, and type of resource, describing real-life applications.

5. The data base can be shared with their peers for future reference.

ACTIVITY 101. SCIENCE IN OUR DAILY LIVES   **OUT OF CLASS / IN CLASS**
                                                               ELEMENTARY SCIENCE

1. Ask your students to keep a log of natural events and phenomena that occur during the semester you are working with them. Examples: a lunar eclipse, an earthquake, flooding, drought, an ice storm, abnormally high or low temperatures, and unusual sunsets. Have them observe, in the field, any natural phenomena possible. Invite them to list any science questions or ideas they have pertaining to the event.

2. Model your discussion of the event with them as a way of using science to make meaning of natural phenomena, integrating "real world" events to foster everyday life connections in the science classroom. Point out that this way of teaching is especially appealing to many girls.

Note: The next six activities model the importance of making connections between science and daily experiences. They can be adapted for mathematics as well, because most involve mathematical processes. They are designed to be experienced by preservice teachers themselves and to be brought into their own teaching environments.

ACTIVITY 102. A SCIENCE FIELD TRIP   **OUT OF CLASS**
                                                               SCIENCE

1. Assign a field trip to your students to help them gain a better understanding of their natural environment and to foster connections between science ideas and the local environment in which the students live.

2. Ask them to write a science lesson from a visit to the beach, a grassy plain, a fresh water pond, a salt marsh, an arboretum, or a canyon, depending on your location. The lesson should include a rationale and the ways in which they would prepare a class for the trip, how they would connect the trip to their course of science study, and what they would expect their students to be doing on the field trip. It should also include the science ideas they want children to gain from the trip and the follow-up activities they would prepare for them on their return.

ACTIVITY 103. PROFOUND SCIENCE WITH FOUND OBJECTS   OUT OF CLASS / IN CLASS
ELEMENTARY SCIENCE

1. Invite students to explore household items that can be used as curriculum materials in elementary science activities: using cooking to change states of matter, doing experiments with corn starch and water, vinegar and baking soda, sugar, salt and talc, corn oil, aluminum foil pie pans, candles, empty juice bottles, mirrors, flashlights, magnets, batteries, and balloons.

2. Challenge students to create their own physical science activities involving principles of changes of state, heat energy, properties of air, properties of water, light energy, sound energy, and electricity with commonly found objects.

3. Discuss their ideas in class.

ACTIVITY 104. HOW DOES IT WORK?   OUT OF CLASS / IN CLASS
ELEMENTARY SCIENCE

1. To reinforce science as a way of making meaning of their world, ask preservice teachers to collect everyday items to "take apart" (i.e. pepper mill, flashlight, transistor radio, can opener, toy car, light-up or buzzing board games, wind-up toy, pencil sharpener, an old small appliance such as a toaster, and so on).

2. Have preservice teachers, working in cooperative learning groups, take apart their items, make a list of the parts and come up with their own ideas about how their selected item works.

ACTIVITY 105. LEARNING ABOUT OUR ENVIRONMENT   OUT OF CLASS / IN CLASS
ELEMENTARY SCIENCE

1. By integrating environmental science in elementary science activities you can help your students gain insight into ways of making science connections for girls in their classrooms. Teach and model any of the following activities:

    *   Start a recycling center.
    *   Visit a resource recovery center.
    *   Visit a water treatment plant.
    *   Visit a garbage dump site!
    *   Make a model of a leaky landfill.
    *   Make a model of an oil spill.
    *   Test for air pollution with vaseline and index cards. (Cover index cards with vaseline and tape to the inside and outside of the classroom window. Examine the cards after four days. On which card is there evidence of more particulate matter? Explore the sources for this pollution.)

ACTIVITY 106. MAKING CONNECTIONS WITH EVERYDAY LIFE IN CLASS

SECONDARY SCIENCE

1. Work with students to use everyday objects wherever possible to enhance the laboratory demonstration:

CHEMISTRY
- Use acids and bases from home, such as vinegar and ammonia
- Use household items and cleansers, such as chlorine bleach, calcium chloride, salt, lemon juice, citric acid
- When studying compounds and mixtures, bring in salt, sugar, vinegar, starch, baking soda, and so on.
- Bring in examples of elements on the periodic table such as gold, silver, copper, nickel, chrome, iron, chlorine, sulfur, aluminum, and so on.

PHYSICS
- Use toys, spring scales, bicycle gears, swinging desk chairs, and so on to illustrate physical principles.

BIOLOGY
- Use indigenous plants from the local environment
- Create a classroom greenhouse

ACTIVITY 107. ENVIRONMENTAL SCIENCE OUT OF CLASS / IN CLASS

SECONDARY SCIENCE

1. Ask students to identify an environmental issue connected with their own science specialty:

- EARTH SCIENCE: air, water or soil pollution, oil spills, global warming, greenhouse effect, wetlands conservation, beach erosion

- PHYSICS: electromagnetic fields and cancer, nuclear power plants

- CHEMISTRY: toxic by-products of production, effects of chlorofluorocarbons on the ozone layer

- BIOLOGY: the introduction of genetically engineered fruits and vegetables, coding the human genome

2. Ask them to write up a lesson plan based on the issue they chose. A good resource is *The Earth Child* by Sheehan & Waidner (see Resources, Volume II).

3. Discuss the importance wherever possible of integrating environmental science issues to activities in biology, chemistry, physics, and especially in earth science.

ACTIVITY 108. DEVELOPING THE CONNECTED LESSON OUT OF CLASS / IN CLASS

1. Ask your students to develop a lesson and write a lesson plan that uses materials, issues or ideas from everyday life. Ask them to indicate the ways in which the ideas behind the lesson connect to daily life.

2. Ask them to demonstrate their lesson for the class.

3. Have them make duplicates for their colleagues for future use.

ACTIVITY 109. PROGRAMMING ACTIVITIES OUT OF CLASS / FIELD
TECHNOLOGY

1. Ask students to research programming activities in the popular computer education magazines such as *Learning and Leading with Technology* (formerly *The Computing Teacher*), *Technology & Learning*, and *Electronic Learning*, and review them for relevance to real-world activities and issues.

2. Ask them to choose an activity that they feel is particularly relevant as well as age-appropriate to do with a class at their field placement school.

3. As they carry out this activity with children, ask your students to note girls' responses to it.

4. Ask students to share with one another the programming activities they use, along with a page or two on their experience in the classroom, suggesting modifications where appropriate. These should be copied and distributed for future classroom use.

ACTIVITY 110. HYPERMEDIA ACTIVITIES OUT OF CLASS / FIELD
TECHNOLOGY

1. Repeat the preceding activity, substituting hypermedia for programming activities.

ACTIVITY 111. USES FOR SPREADSHEETS IN CLASS / FIELD
TECHNOLOGY

1. In a class discussion, invite students to create a list of uses for spreadsheets in every day life. These may include:

• Personal and family budgeting

- Determining the minimum salary a person needs to earn to cover expenses
- Comparing the cost of buying a car to that of leasing it or taking public transportation
- Determining the total cost of a mortgage
- Modifying a recipe to make more or less than originally intended
- Preparing a budget for a project or a proposal

2. Ask students to carry out one or more of their spreadsheet ideas with children in their field placement schools.

ACTIVITY 112. TECHNOLOGY IN THE WORLD   **IN CLASS / FIELD**

TECHNOLOGY

1. In a class discussion, invite students to brainstorm a list of the ways they see technology working in their lives. The list may include: automatic teller machines, laser code readers at grocery store checkouts, automated telephone information services, telephone answering machines, microwave ovens, automatic cameras, and so on.

2. In their field placement classes, students ask children which ones they know how to use themselves, and note any differences between girls' and boys' responses. How can what they learn help them to develop technology learning activities?

ACTIVITY 113. CHILDREN CARRY OUT A SURVEY   **FIELD**

TECHNOLOGY

1. Ask your students to read "Guidelines for a Children's Survey" on page 49, Volume II:

   a. *Invite the students to break into small working groups. Each group chooses a topic relevant to themselves and their peers on which to base a survey. Topics can be anything of interest chosen by the group.*

   b. *Each group designs and administers its survey and decides how the computer can be used in the process. Students can use word processors or desktop publishing programs to prepare survey forms, and spreadsheets, graphics programs, and graphing programs to represent their findings. Advanced students can use a statistical analysis program to analyze their data.*

   c. *Invite students to share their findings with one another, either by preparing copies of their results for everyone or using them in a bulletin board.*

2. Ask your students to discuss their experience with this activity in their regular field seminar, paying special attention to girls' level of participation and involvement.

ACTIVITY 114. TECHNOLOGY AS TOOL   **FIELD / IN CLASS**

TECHNOLOGY

1. Ask students to work with a teacher in their field placement schools to create a curriculum-specific lesson (in math, social studies, art, and so on.) that uses technology as a tool. Educational computing magazines offer many suggestions. Possibilities include telecommunications, multimedia, databases, spreadsheets, and desktop publishing.

2. In class, ask them to share their activities with one another.

3E. BIASED LANGUAGE IN CURRICULAR MATERIALS

Our choice of words conveys our biases and assumptions about the world around us, and the idea that mathematics, science, and technology are for males and not for females is embedded in many curriculum materials, especially older ones. When we accept the language, we accept the idea as well. Pre-service teachers need to become aware of language biases as they review and select materials for their classes.

ACTIVITY 115. INTERVIEW A COOPERATING TEACHER   FIELD / IN CLASS

1. Ask students to interview their cooperating teacher or science coordinator to determine how many teachers or science supervisors use the criterion "use of non-sexist language" when selecting a textbook or other written instructional material (i.e. lab manuals and supplements).

2. Review the results in class.

ACTIVITY 116. ENVISIONING LANGUAGE   IN CLASS

1. Ask students to close their eyes for a moment while you say a word, and to picture in their mind's eye the image the word suggests.

2. Say a word or phrase such as "guy," "the man in the street," "a caveman," or "the common man."

3. Ask students about the image they "saw" — did it have a skirt on or not? Discuss the implications for girls in school, not necessarily every time they hear a male generic term but cumulatively over years.

ACTIVITY 117. ASSIGNED READING I   OUT OF CLASS / IN CLASS

1. Ask students to read the research indicating that biased language in science discourages people from visualizing women in scientific roles. If you teach mathematics methods or technology methods, suggest that your students draw the parallel to mathematicians and technologists. Recommended are:

    • Chapter 2, "Feminist Theories and Methods," in *Female-Friendly Science* by Sue Rosser.

- "Is the Subject of Science Sexed?" by Luce Irigaray from *Feminism and Science* edited by Nancy Tuana (see Volume II, Resources, for information on both).

2. Ask them to look for newspaper reports and journal and magazine articles that refer to scientists, mathematicians and technologists by first as well as last names, enabling females to become visible in these materials. Discuss the readings and their sample articles.

ACTIVITY 118. ASSIGNED READING II   **OUT OF CLASS / IN CLASS**

1. Ask students to read two chapters in *Metamagical Themas* by Douglas Hofstadter, the former editor of a *Scientific American* column (see Resources, Volume II). The first is Chapter 7, "Changes in Default Words and Images, Engendered by Rising Consciousness," which is a wonderful piece on how gender-biased language shapes and limits our thinking. Especially powerful is Chapter 8, "A Person Paper on Purity in Language" in which Hofstadter creates a pseudo-linguistic structure that reflects not gender as our language does (e.g., *her* and *his*) but race. What's wrong, he asks ironically, with pronouns that refer to white and black people, perfectly good words such as *chairwhite, straw white,* and *middlewhite*? Powerful and highly recommended.

2. Ask students to discuss their reactions to these two chapters.

ACTIVITY 119. LANGUAGE IN CURRICULUM MATERIALS   **OUT OF CLASS**

1. Ask students to read "Guidelines for Nonsexist Use of Language" from the National Council of Teachers of English (Volume II, pages 50-53).

2. Ask students to review several textbooks, software programs, or other curriculum materials, examining them for each type of language bias identified in the reprint.

3. Require that all papers for your course be written in gender-fair language. You might want to recommend (or require) that students purchase a copy of one of these two inexpensive paperback reference books:

- Dumond, Val (1990). *The Elements of Nonsexist Usage: A Guide to Inclusive Spoken and Written English.* New York: Prentice Hall.

- Schwartz, Marilyn and the Association of American University Presses (1995). *Guidelines for Bias-Free Writing.* Bloomington, IN: Indiana University Press.

1. Ask students to explore textbooks for the use of the generic *he* to mean *he and she* and for use of terms such as *mankind* for *humankind* and *man* for *people*. Ask them to report on their findings by indicating the number of times the incorrect terms are used for a given chapter or text.

2. Ask them to find other gender-inappropriate usages. How would they correct the language problems they cite?

3F. MATERIALS FOSTER ISOLATED, COMPETITIVE ACTIVITIES

Research shows that girls often prefer working in collaboration with others as opposed to working individually or in competition with others. When curriculum materials foster isolated, competitive work, girls are more likely to lose interest. This can influence their decisions to continue working with and learning about mathematics, science and technology. Preservice teachers need to identify these aspects of learning materials and find alternatives.

ACTIVITY 121. ACADEMIC COMPETITIONS   **IN CLASS**

1. Hold a class discussion on academic competitions, which students may be familiar with either from their own elementary and secondary school years or from their field placement experience. They can read "Gender and Mathematics Contests" by Rosalie Nichols and Ray Kurtz (see Resources, Volume II).

2. Ask questions such as:

   - Should girls be encouraged to participate in academic competitions?
   - Why or why not?
   - If not, what are the implications for boys who participate?
   - If so, how would you encourage girls to participate?
   - Are there ways you might change the rules to make competitions more attractive to girls? (E.g., have pairs or teams compete rather than individuals)
   - Are there other aspects of school life that foster competitiveness between the sexes? Do they matter?

ACTIVITY 122. SOFTWARE ANXIETY   **IN CLASS**
                                                                              TECHNOLOGY

1. Bring several software packages to class. The assortment should include both timed, competitive programs, such as *Math Shop* (in the scoring mode), *Number Maze* or *Number Munchers*, and non-competitive programs such as *Kid Pix*, *Pow Zap Kerplunk*, and *Arthur's Teacher Trouble*.

2. Have some students work in groups and some individually. Assign both types of software to each type of group.

3. Make a chart on the board:

	Group		Individual	
Software	Female	Male	Female	Male
Competitive				
Non-competitive				

4. Ask each student where she or he fits on the chart, and ask them how they felt when working with their software. Write a U for each person who was uncomfortable, and an N for each person who was not. Do any patterns emerge?

ACTIVITY 123. FEMALE STYLES OF LEARNING   OUT OF CLASS / FIELD / IN CLASS
MATHEMATICS

1. Ask students to read "Women's Learning Styles and the Teaching of Mathematics" by Judith Jacobs (see Resources, Volume II).

2. Ask them to observe a class to determine how girls and boys come to knowledge.

3. In class, discuss the research and the implications for planning effective instruction. Be sure that the discussion addresses variations in learning styles within each sex. Females and males are not different species!

4. Students write sample lesson plans focusing on the research and observations, such as children constructing knowledge of a specific mathematics topic.

5. Students share their plans with the class or teach the lessons to their classmates.

ACTIVITY 124. AN EQUITABLE CURRICULUM MODEL   IN CLASS

1. Ask students to read "Equitable Science And Mathematics Education: A Discrepancy Model" by Jane Butler Kahle and Marsha Lakes Matyas (see Resources, Volume II, for the full reference).

2. After class discussion, have students select one of the points made in the reading and create a data base or list of materials, books and so on that support an issue from the model. For example in mathematics, for the equity issue: "Activities that foster cooperative, rather than competitive, investigations," resources could include:

- Burns, Marilyn (1987). *A Collection of Math Lessons*
- Burns, Marilyn (1977). *The Good Time Math Event Book* (see Resources, Volume II, for both).

3. The data bases or lists can then be shared among students and kept for future reference.

EQUITY ISSUE 4

CLASSROOM INTERACTION AND ATMOSPHERE

When teachers have biased beliefs, research has repeatedly and conclusively shown that they inadvertently express them to their students in the form of biased behaviors. This is true of both women and men. Small and often subtle behaviors favoring males by teachers and — permitted by teachers — classmates, which can include a competitive or aggressive classroom atmosphere, serve to discourage girls and young women from continuing in mathematics, science and technology. While each individual incident may be trivial, the accumulation of biased incidents is powerful. Often girls themselves do not realize the source of their discouragement. Only by identifying problem behaviors can they be eliminated.

4A. BIASED TEACHER/STUDENT INTERACTIONS

Many teachers inadvertently favor boys in their classroom behavior. Research shows that especially in male-dominated subjects such as mathematics, science, and technology, teachers call on boys more often than girls, wait longer for boys' answers, and engage boys when they call out, while reprimanding girls and reminding them to raise their hands. Research also shows that when teachers receive training in unbiased classroom behaviors and feedback on their own behavior, these imbalances can be corrected. Preservice teachers need to examine their own behavior before they begin their teaching careers.

ACTIVITY 125. WHAT THE RESEARCH SAYS   **OUT OF CLASS /IN CLASS**

---

1. Ask students to read the research on gender-biased classroom interactions using any or all of these resources:

   - Sandler, Bernice et al (1996). *The Chilly Classroom Climate: A Guide to Improve the Education of Women.*

   - Sandler, Bernice (1991). "Warming Up the Chilly Climate" *in Math and Science for Girls,* pages 26-41.

- American Association of University Women (1992). "The Classroom as Curriculum" in *How Schools Shortchange Girls*, pages 68-74; Marlowe & Co. edition, 1995, pages 119-131.

- Grossman, Herbert, and Grossman, and Suzanne. (1994). "Reducing Gender-Stereotypical Behavior" in *Gender Issues in Education*, pages 167-190 (see Resources, Volume II, for all).

2. Hand out "Gender-Biased Student/Teacher Interactions," page 54 of Volume II, as a summary of the research.

3. Discuss the research in class with reference to the following points:

- Boys are called on to answer questions more frequently than girls.
- Boys are coached when they give an incorrect answer. Girls are passed over when they answer wrong.
- Boys are praised for the content of their work. Girls are praised for their neatness.
- Boys are called on to handle science equipment and set-up. Girls are called on to clean up.
- Teachers coach boys to complete a science activity while doing it for the girls.
- Teachers allow girls to opt out of doing certain science activities, while encouraging boys to complete the tasks.
- Teachers have greater expectations for boys in science than for girls.

ACTIVITY 126. INSTRUCTIONAL VIDEO, BEFORE AND AFTER   **YOUR TIME / IN CLASS**

1. You probably already show to your students one or more instructional videotapes showing experienced teachers in typical classroom situations. If not, ask colleagues for recommendations.

2. Watch the videotape yourself, but this time for gender equity interactions as covered in this section. Use the handout from the preceding activity as a guide in what to watch for. You will probably (but not certainly) find inadvertent gender-biased behavior on the teacher's part and among the students' as well.

3. Early in the semester show the videotape to students in the usual way, without mentioning gender equity. Ask them to note down any observations they think are important as they watch the tape. Announce each minute that passes to enable them to have a time marker for their observations.

4. Later in the semester after gender equity has been thoroughly introduced, show the videotape again and repeat Step 3. This time around students should spot the bias examples very quickly.

5. Hold a discussion about the difference between students' pre- and post-observations.

ACTIVITY 127. PRACTICE CODING   **IN CLASS**

1. Choose a coding form from among those provided for students in Volume II on pages 55-60. We have provided five at different levels of complexity, so choose the one you think your students would do best with.

2. To give your students practice in coding classroom interactions, choose an easily observable interaction, such as when you call on a student or accept her or his called-out answer. Hold a discussion on any topic you like. Suggest that students keep their comments relatively short to provide more codable opportunities.

3. Keep the discussion going for five to ten minutes, then ask students about their results. If you have a sex imbalance in your class, point out or ask students what the equitable ratio would be.

4. Tell them that they can use this method to observe and quantify student/teacher interactions in their other university classes as well as their field placement classes, and they can use it for a variety of behaviors. Emphasize that gender-biased behavior is inadvertent and nondeliberate, that women as well as men do it, and if people are unaware of what they are doing blame is not an appropriate response. (See the next activity for how people can become aware of what they are doing and change their behavior.)

5. Students can use a coding form of their choice from those provided in Volume II or create their own. If classroom observations are to be a group project, however, it will be essential for comparability purposes for all students to use the same form.

ACTIVITY 128. SURVEY OF CLASSROOM INTERACTIONS   **FIELD / OUT OF CLASS / IN CLASS**

1. Ask your students to arrange to observe a mathematics, science, or technology teacher in their field placement school three times about a week apart, using one of the coding forms in Volume II. Each student should choose a single behavior to be observed all three times. Students should ask the teacher if she or he would like to receive the results of the observations, and if so this should be provided confidentially and factually to the teacher, with no value judgments.

2. Ask students to write a summary of their findings, with particular attention to whether the teacher's gender-related behavior changed across the observations as a function of being given the observation results. Typically, teachers do change toward more equitable behavior after receiving the results of two to four observation sessions.

3. Hold a discussion on what students found. How can biased — or equitable — interactions influence children's expectations, and ultimately, their achievements?

ACTIVITY 129. OBSERVING UNIVERSITY CLASSROOMS   **OUT OF CLASS / IN CLASS**

1. With everyone using the same coding form chosen from among those provided in Volume II, have students select classes at your university or college to observe for teacher/student interaction patterns. Be sure there is a good mix of physical science and humanities classes, because those are the most stereotypically male and female. They can also include the social sciences, which tend to be more neutral.

2. Students should pool their results, taking care to omit the names of professors they observed to avoid personalizing their findings. Hold a discussion in class on the findings and the implications.

ACTIVITY 130. JOURNALS AND SELF-OBSERVATIONS   **OUT OF CLASS**

1. After teaching any of the preceding activities on this topic, ask your students to begin a personal journal reflecting on their beliefs and self-observations concerning their own biased and nonbiased teaching behaviors.

ACTIVITY 131. VIDEOTAPING CLASSROOM BEHAVIOR   **FIELD / IN CLASS / OUT OF CLASS**

1. Ask your students to have themselves videotaped in their field placements as they teach a lesson. If you prefer, have all students in your class videotaped as they practice-teach a lesson to each other.

2. To analyze the tapes: 1) have each student privately analyze her or his own tape for selected teacher/student interaction patterns, or 2) have each student analyze someone else's tape, or 3) have the entire class analyze together a sample of the tapes. They can use any of the five coding forms provided in Volume II, pages 55-60.

3. If you choose Option 1, ask students to write an analysis of what they learned from observing their own taped teaching and what they plan to do differently. If Option 2, ask students to write a short essay on what they learned from the results of the observation and what they plan to do differently. If Option 3, hold a class discussion on the patterns they are seeing and what can be done to change them.

ACTIVITY 132. VIGNETTE: MS. MARCUS' FIFTH-GRADE CLASS   **IN CLASS**
                                                                             SCIENCE

1. Distribute the following vignette to your students. Duplicate it from Volume II, page 61.

    Ms. Marcus' fifth-grade class is making presentations to the class on inventors.

    She asks who wants to go first. Deirdre raises her hand and gives her presentation about two chemists who became famous cosmetologists: Madame C. J. Walker and Helena Rubinstein. She displays a poster showing some of the chemical processes required to make face cream. Her presentation lasts seven minutes. There are no questions, but everyone applauds and she sits down.

    Ronald goes next. He is dressed in a white lab coat and he talks about Charles Drew, who invented the blood bank system. He also has posters with him, and his presentation lasts 15 minutes. Ms. Marcus asks him several probing questions, and then the class asks other questions. Ronald is in front of the class 25 minutes before he sits down.

    If you were Ms. Marcus, what would you do about the unequal time children have for their presentations?

2. Ask students to discuss the case study in small groups.

ACTIVITY 133. AUTOBIOGRAPHIES   **OUT OF CLASS / IN CLASS**

1. Invite your students to write an essay reviewing their own school experiences in science, mathematics, or technology. Were they ever subjected to sex-biased treatment or attitudes about their achievement in these subjects from teachers or other students? Was there any difference in how they were treated in elementary and secondary grades? A resource is:

    - Koch, Janice (1990). "The Science Autobiography Project." (See Resources, Volume II.)

2. Conduct a class discussion on their conclusions.

ACTIVITY 134. GENDER DIFFERENCES AT THE COMPUTER   **FIELD**
                                                                       SECONDARY TECHNOLOGY

1. Ask your students to observe a high school computing class where students are working at computers. Have them write their observations to the following questions:

    a. Do girls or boys ask for help more often?
    b. Do the student tend to wait for help from the teacher or ask another student? Does this vary by sex?

c. Are they asking for help with problem solving or syntax? Does this vary by sex?

d. Are there students who refuse help because they want to "do it themselves"? Does this vary by sex?

2. The observer should note differences in behavior among males and females.

ACTIVITY 135. EXAMINING A PHYSICS CLASSROOM   IN CLASS

1. Show your students the videotape from NBC's *Dateline* show with Jane Pauley (February 9, 1994) in which a teacher taught co-ed and same-sex sections of his physics class.

2. Conduct a discussion of the attributes of the two classes, with particular attention to the teacher/student interactions.

3. What conclusions, if any, may be drawn from this experiment?

ACTIVITY 136. ROLE-PLAY BIASED AND UNBIASED INTERACTIONS   IN CLASS

1. Assign roles to your students. Here are some possible roles; you can make up others as you choose.

    *   Shy girl, knows a lot about MST, doesn't volunteer knowledge
    *   Social girl, wants to interact with others
    *   Aggressive boy, knows a lot about MST, wants to show what he knows
    *   Shy boy, likes MST
    *   Shy girl, doesn't like MST
    *   Class clown boy
    *   Class clown girl
    *   Teacher

2. Conduct a short mock class, with the "teacher" exhibiting one of the following biased behaviors:

    *   Calling on boys more than girls
    *   Accepting boys' called-out answers more than girls'
    *   Asking boys more interpretive questions, girls more factual ones
    *   Waiting longer for boys' answers than for girls'
    *   Giving girls neutral responses ("Okay") and boys more complex responses, both positive and negative
    *   Positioning the body toward boys more than girls
    *   Circulating more to boys' desks than girls' desks
    *   Telling boys how to solve problems but solving problems for girls

3. The role play can be conducted as many times as you like, each time demonstrating a different biased behavior.

4. Lead a discussion of the class, encouraging your students to identify biased behaviors and suggest alternatives.

5. Ask students to take turns conducting mock lessons that apply some of the nonbiased approaches they have discussed.

4B. PHYSICAL ENVIRONMENT

The physical design and affective climate of the classroom can influence collaborative or isolated student activities. How a classroom is set up in terms of student groupings, accessibility of equipment and materials, bulletin boards, and seating arrangements can subtly encourage or discourage participation in classroom activities. Because group work and peer teaching are conducive to greater female participation, arranging a classroom to favor these activities encourages the creation of more "female-friendly" interactive environments.

ACTIVITY 137. OBSERVING A CLASSROOM   FIELD / IN CLASS

1. Have your students observe one or more classrooms in their field placement school and make notes on the physical environment they observe. Suggestions for observation:

    - Seating patterns

        Are students seated according to sex?
        Are the girls in the front of the room, back of the room?
        Are chairs arranged in rows or clusters?

    - Grouping patterns

        Are informal or teacher-directed groups set up by sex?
        Are furniture arrangements flexible? Are they ever changed for different learning purposes?

    - Materials or equipment

        Does everyone have equal access in actual fact to the materials?
        Who uses, distributes, and collects the materials?
        If some materials or equipment are scarce resources, who gets to use them most?

    - Bulletin boards

        Which sex is displayed on the subject-specific bulletin boards?
        Which sex is displayed on other illustrations in the room?
        Are there pictures of women in nontraditional roles?

    - Monitors

        Are girls asked to do nontraditional classroom chores?

    - Line-up (elementary)

        Are students lined up separately by sex?
        Are students lined up "ladies first"?

2. Students report their observations during a group discussion, noting what they would do the same way and what they would do differently.

ACTIVITY 138. BULLETIN BOARDS AND SUCH   FIELD / IN CLASS

1. Ask students to visit many classrooms in their field placement schools and take notes on what they see on the walls. What proportion of females and males do the bulletin boards, posters, and other materials affixed to the walls show? Do these proportions vary by grade level? Do they vary by subject?

2. Ask students to report in class on what they found. If they found many bulletin boards in math, science and technology classes that showed all or nearly all males, would they rather see additional bulletin boards devoted exclusively to females or the existing bulletin boards show males and females equally? Why?

ACTIVITY 139. DESIGNING A CLASSROOM   OUT OF CLASS

1. Using a computer or pencil and graph paper, ask students to make a scale drawing of a classroom that would promote equity, taking into account student grouping for different learning purposes, manipulatives and materials, and equipment.

2. Ask students to write a rationale for their design addressing the equity issues.

4C. PEER AGGRESSIVENESS

Research has shown that males receive more attention and, therefore, more help during MST lessons in part because they show more aggressive behaviors than females. Aggressiveness is culturally sanctioned behavior for boys —"Boys will be boys!" — and can often be physical in elementary grades and verbal in secondary grades. Commonly it shows up when teachers fail to stop boys (or occasionally girls) who make aggressive or hostile comments or exhibit such behaviors to female classmates or quieter male classmates. When girls don't feel safe from ridicule in expressing their opinions or answering questions, they learn not to venture opinions or answers in class. A silent, withdrawn student is likely to believe that she is not very good at mathematics, science, or technology, which can become a self-fulfilling prophecy. Preservice teachers need to be able to identify and deal constructively with aggressive male behavior and be aware of behaviors that will encourage female success.

ACTIVITY 140. OBSERVE STUDENT BEHAVIOR   FIELD / IN CLASS

1. In class, ask students to create a list of aggressive — different from assertive! — classroom behaviors they have witnessed or remember personally from their own grade school years. How do they remember feeling about these behaviors?

2. Ask your students to observe a class at their field placement over several sessions, watching for aggressive behavior on the boys' part as well as the girls' responses. In elementary classrooms, do boys grab the math manipulatives, computers, or science equipment? How do girls respond? In secondary classrooms physical aggressiveness may be less likely, but verbal aggressiveness may be more potent. Do boys tease or humiliate girls when they try to contribute to an activity? What do the girls do in response? What are the responses of the quiet boys to the behavior of aggressive boys?

3. Ask students to write a brief paper on their observations.

4. Hold a discussion in class on students' observations. What patterns did they see? Are there any cultural or ethnic factors that might be relevant among the children they observed? What should a teacher do in such situations?

ACTIVITY 141. EAVESDROPPING   FIELD / OUT OF CLASS

1. Ask students to listen in the cafeteria or hallway of their field placement school and count the "put-downs" they hear, in terms of the sex to which they are addressed or about which sex they refer to. Have them also record the amount of observation time they spend.

2. Ask them to write their findings in a brief essay, and to reflect on the meaning of what they found in terms of girls' (and boys') learning environment.

ACTIVITY 142. CASE STUDY: NCTM STANDARDS   IN CLASS

MATHEMATICS

1. Distribute section 3.3 of NCTM Professional Teaching Standards/Professional Development, pages 149-150.

2. After reading the situation described in the material, discuss with your students strategies that answer the question, *"What are some alternatives for this teacher?"*

ACTIVITY 143. ANECDOTAL OBSERVATIONS   FIELD / IN CLASS

1. Ask students to observe a male student and a female student in the same class during several lessons. The students should be comparable in ability.

2. Ask them to keep an anecdotal record of the students' behavior, attitude, and performance during each lesson.

3. Have them present their findings to the class, and have the group note any differences in behaviors between female and male students observed.

ACTIVITY 144. SCENARIO: YOU ARE TEACHING YOUR CLASS   IN CLASS

1. Ask students to refer to the scenario on page 62, Volume II.

You are teaching your class and have just called on Junie to answer a question. She looks confused. Before Junie has a chance to say anything, Mark mutters loudly enough for everyone to hear, "She'll never get it — she's an airhead."

You could:

- *Ignore the comment.*
- *Disagree, saying that Junie isn't stupid at all.*
- *Agree, saying that after all, Junie is trying hard.*
- *Reprimand Mark mildly.*
- *Reprimand Mark harshly.*

- *Tell Mark to leave your class and return only when he can be civil.*
- *Hold a class discussion on insulting behavior.*

Consider the consequences for Junie, Mark, and the rest of the class of various courses of action open to you. What is the best thing you can do?

2. Have students discuss the scenario in groups of three.

ACTIVITY 145. INTERVIEWING TEACHERS   **FIELD / OUT OF CLASS**

1. Have students arrange to interview two or three teachers at their field placement schools. Interview questions might include:

   - Have you observed any of the following behaviors in your classes:

     - Boys pushing girls away from equipment, manipulatives, or computers
     - Girls pushing boys away from equipment, manipulatives, or computers
     - Boys teasing girls about their ideas or work
     - Girls teasing boys about their ideas or work

   - Have you noticed students withdrawing from activities as a result of physical or verbal aggressiveness? If so, are girls more likely to withdraw, or are boys?

2. Ask them to write a brief paper on their interviews and share them with one another. Do any patterns emerge?

ACTIVITY 146. BUILDING TOWERS   **FIELD / OUT OF CLASS / IN CLASS**

1. Students ask children in their field placement classes to form mixed (boys and girls) groups of four. Students distribute index cards to each group; alternatively, blocks could be used for younger children. The groups' task is to build the highest tower they can in 10 minutes. Each group should choose one person to report their best tower-building strategy to the class.

2. Your students should observe the groups for gender interactions.

3. For homework, students write the answers to three directions:

   - Describe what you saw: verbal and nonverbal interactions, roles in the group.
   - Interpret it.
   - Create a plan to improve the gender interactions in a mixed-group, hands-on activity.

4. Hold a discussion in class on what they learned.

**4D. INSTRUCTIONAL STRATEGIES DO NOT FOSTER
COOPERATIVE LEARNING AND COLLABORATION**

Research shows that many, if not most, females, as well as a sizeable proportion of males, learn best in a cooperative, social, and collaborative environment. This is, of course, the environment in which most scientists, mathematicians, and technologists actually work. To the extent that the educational process or environment reflects isolated or competitive modes of learning and relating, we can expect that a number of girls will be unnecessarily disadvantaged. There are many ways that cooperative learning and collaborations can be used in the teaching and learning of mathematics, science, and technology.

ACTIVITY 147. WHAT THE RESEARCH SAYS   **OUT OF CLASS**

1. Ask students to review the research on cooperative learning as it pertains to gender equity. Recommended is:

   • Dillow, Karen et al. (1994). "Cooperative Learning and the Achievement of Female Students"

ACTIVITY 148. OBSERVING COOPERATIVE GROUPS   **FIELD / IN CLASS**

1. Cooperative groups are not automatically gender-fair. Have your students observe children in their field placement classes when cooperative group activities are occurring. Suggest that they observe for the following issues, which are presented on page 63 in Volume II.

   1. *What is the gender composition and the size of the group(s) they are observing? What is its task?*
   2. *Who is the group's leader, if there is one? How has this been decided?*
   3. *How are the roles allocated among group members? How has this been decided?*
   4. *Does everyone get a chance to do each role? If not, who (male or female) does which task?*
   5. *Does everyone contribute equally to the group's work? If not, who (male or female) contributes most and who least?*
   6. *Does everyone speak equally in the group? If not, who (male or female) speaks most and who least?*
   7. *Does everyone have equal use of any equipment or other resources? If not, who (male or female) has most use and who least?*
   8. *Does the teacher intervene in group functioning? Why, how, and with what results?*
   9. *Do group dynamics differ according to whether they are single-sex or mixed-sex?*
   10. *What techniques could be used by a teacher to prevent inequitable group dynamics and promote equitable ones?*

2. In a class discussion, ask students to report on what they saw and the conclusions they drew. Ask them what factors seemed to lead to equitable groups and which seemed to produce inequitable groups. Stress that cooperative groups may or may not be equitable depending on the dynamics of the group.

3. Ask students what they as teachers could do to prevent any inequitable dynamics they observed in the groups from occurring.

ACTIVITY 149. A LESSON FOR COOPERATIVE GROUPS   **OUT OF CLASS / FIELD**

1. Ask your students to write a lesson plan that uses cooperative learning, designing cooperative learning groups where female students assume a fair share of the active roles in the group and do not just record the group's work.

2. If possible have them teach and videotape their lesson in field placement classes, or present it to classmates in methods class. How well did their lesson plan work out?

ACTIVITY 150. TECHNOLOGY VIGNETTES   **OUT OF CLASS**

     TECHNOLOGY

1. Ask students to write their response to this two-part vignette on technology, which is included in Volume II on page 64:

   A. *You are teaching in a well equipped computer lab. Each student has his or her own computer and is working alone. You notice that many of the girls in the class seem to be bored. You know that girls are often happier working in groups, so you assign all your students to mixed-sex groups and ask them to continue their work collaboratively.*

   Is this approach likely to be successful? Why or why not?

   B. *You now notice that the girls in the groups you have assigned are the secretaries and errand-runners, while the boys are making the decisions and doing the actual work at the computers.*

   What do you do?

2. Remind students that according to Title IX, segregating students by sex in public schools is almost always illegal, so they need to find other solutions.

ACTIVITY 151. PEER INTERACTION IN THE SCIENCE LAB   FIELD / IN CLASS

SCIENCE

1. Ask your students to observe a science lab experience at either the elementary or the secondary level.

2. Ask them to write up an observational analysis responding to the following:

    - How are the students grouped for lab (single sex, coed)?
    - Who sets up the materials? Who cleans up after the lab?
    - What are the boys doing with materials? The girls?
    - What similarities and differences in behavior do you notice between the girls and boys?

    What indications, if any, do you observe of dominant and passive behavior?

3. If possible, have them visit an all girls' science lab and compare results.

4. Ask students to brainstorm how teachers can set up a gender-equitable environment in a coed science lab.

ACTIVITY 152. PEER TEACHING   IN CLASS

ELEMENTARY SCIENCE

1. Divide your students into pairs.

2. Give a different science content module to each individual. For example: units on heat energy, light energy, electricity and magnetism, types and states of matter, simple machines, rocks and minerals, seeds and plants, invertebrates and vertebrates, and so on. For units, the following book is good (see Volume II, Resources):

    - Gega, Peter (1993). *Concepts and Experiences in Elementary Science.*

3. Have pairs teach each other what they learned from their modules. Then have them re-pair and work with a different learning partner to teach each other the material.

4. Ask students to write a paper reacting to the peer teaching experience. In what ways was it beneficial? What were the problems?

ACTIVITY 153. SAME-SCIENCE DISCIPLINE TEAMS   IN CLASS / OUT OF CLASS

SECONDARY SCIENCE

1. Divide your students by discipline teams — biology, chemistry, physics, and earth science.

2. Have each team identify an environmental issue related to their area and ask them to define a problem, collect data, analyze data, and present results to the class in a variety of modes. Presentations can include role-playing dramatizations, pictorializations, videotapes, or others.

3. Give each group a group grade, or ask groups to grade themselves, for presentations alone or for presentations and a group report.

4. Ask students to write an individual reflection paper assessing this mode of group work for its benefits and potential problems.

EQUITY ISSUE 5

ANTI-INTELLECTUALISM AND ATTRIBUTIONAL STYLE

One reason gender differences exist in performance and participation in mathematics, science, and technology is because of the lack of females' confidence when doing them. Achievement motivation, attributional style, and pressures from society can contribute to a lack of confidence and a fear of success. Some teaching behaviors toward girls and women can encourage a learned helplessness which further reduces confidence and eventually results in the loss of self-esteem. Traditional female characteristics of helplessness and risk avoidance are incompatible with forthright intellectual achievement in MST, and achievement is considered a fluke rather than earned. This belief is unfortunately strengthened by anti-intellectual currents in mainstream American society. Preservice teachers need to recognize these influences and learn how to counteract them.

5A. ATTRIBUTIONAL STYLE: GIRLS ARE LUCKY AND BOYS ARE SMART

Research shows that there tends to be a difference in how boys and girls interpret their successes and failures. Boys typically attribute their successes to their own intelligence and their failures to insufficient effort. Many girls believe their successes are due to luck and their failures to inability. When girls fail, there is no motivation to try again: trying harder or risking a new approach won't make much difference if you're simply not very good at the subject at hand. Girls need to know that they can apply their intelligence effectively in the area of math, science, and technology, or they will be discouraged from continuing.

ACTIVITY 154. WHAT THE RESEARCH SAYS   OUT OF CLASS

1. Assign one or more of the following articles on how attribution theory relates to gender, particularly for mathematics, science, and technology. Full cites for all are in Resources, Volume II.

   • Eccles, J. S. (1994). "Understanding Women's Educational and Occupational Choices: Applying the Eccles et al. Model of Achievement-Related Choices."

   • Eccles, J. S. (1987). "Gender Roles and Women's Achievement-Related Decisions."

94

- Eccles, J. S. (1989). "Bringing Young Women to Math and Science."

- Eccles (Parsons), J. et al. (1982). "Sex Differences in Attributions and Learned Helplessness."

- Steinberg, Adria (1994). "When Bright Kids Get Bad Grades."

- Bornholt, Laurel et al. (1994). "Influences of Gender Stereotypes on Adolescents' Perceptions of Their Own Achievement."

ACTIVITY 155. INTERVIEWS WITH CHILDREN   **FIELD / IN CLASS**

1. Have your students interview male and female elementary and/or secondary students in their field placement classes by asking them to complete the statement,

    "I am a good math / science / technology student because . . ."

2. Students work in pairs or groups to discuss the responses and identify the attributional styles indicated by the children.

3. Students compare the results of boys and girls.

ACTIVITY 156. FIELD OBSERVATIONS   **FIELD / IN CLASS**

1. Ask students to observe girls' behavior in science class when they have completed a test and when they receive it back, and to contrast this to boys' behavior around tests and grades.

2. In class, explain attribution theory: Girls are more likely to attribute their success to luck, boys are more likely to attribute their success to ability. In other words, girls' locus of control tends to be unstable and unreliable — such as they think they studied especially hard this time, while boys' locus of control tends to be stable and predictable — such as they think they are good test takers. Competent females tend to have higher expectations of failure and lower self-confidence when encountering new academic situations than do boys with similar abilities. Girls tend to attribute their failures to lack of ability while boys attribute their failures to external circumstances such as an unfair test or sudden illness.

3. Ask students about their classroom observations in light of your discussion of attribution theory.

ACTIVITY 157. DEFINING ATTRIBUTIONAL STYLES   **OUT OF CLASS**

1.   Have students research and prepare a written report on attributional styles of learning:

   - Internal (e.g., self-directed) vs. external (e.g., teacher-directed)
   - Stable (predictable) vs. unstable (unpredictable)
   - Controllable vs. uncontrollable (by the student)

In addition to the references earlier in this section, students can read:

   - Kloosterman, Peter (1990). "Attributions, Performance Following Failure, and Motivation in Mathematics" in *Mathematics and Gender*, (Eds.) Elizabeth Fennema and Gilah C. Leder.
   - Tobias, Sheila (1993). *Overcoming Math Anxiety*, 2nd edition.
   - Riesz, Elizabeth D., et al. (1994). "Gender Differences in High School Students' Attitudes Toward Science: Research and Intervention" in *Journal of Women and Minorities in Science and Engineering*. (Full cites in Resources, Volume II.)

ACTIVITY 158. SCENARIO: MR. CHANG   **OUT OF CLASS**

                                                       ELEMENTARY MATHEMATICS

1.   Ask your students to refer to the scenario on page 65, Volume II, and ask them to submit a written response.

        Mr. Chang, a sixth grade teacher, has noticed that one of his female students, Sara, was beginning to give up working on mathematics problems if she did not get the answer on her first attempt. Most of the time, Sara's mathematics assignments are complete and she has the right answers, but Mr. Chang is noticing that Sara is becoming unwilling to try new approaches if she gets an incorrect response. This attitude is especially noticeable on open-ended tasks where strategy is important in getting the solution. He believes this is due to a lack of confidence in mathematics and Sara's belief that her ability is due to chance and not effort.

        During the last lesson, Mr. Chang gave the class the following problem:

            Suppose five people meet at a family party and that each
            person shakes hands with each of the other people once.
            How many handshakes will there be?

Sara gave the answer of 15 handshakes.

        When Mr. Chang asked Sara to explain how she arrived at the answer, Sara said that she made a lucky guess. Mr. Chang feels this is a critical time in Sara's mathematics education and wants to build Sara's confidence.

What could Mr. Chang do to help Sara realize that her ability to reason mathematically enables her to explore math activities and that the answers do not come by chance?

ACTIVITY 159. ACADEMIC CHOICES   **IN CLASS**

1. Refer your students to:

    •   "General Model of Achievement Choices" by Jacquelynne Eccles (reprinted on page 66 in Volume II).

2. Discuss the model in class and ask students to consider specific strategies or approaches that they can use as teachers to deal with the factors that ultimately affect girls' subject choices.

ACTIVITY 160. TIMELINE   **FIELD**
                                                                                   TECHNOLOGY

1. Remind your students that sometimes girls don't realize they know a great deal about using a computer even if the software is not one with which they are familiar. This activity enables them to reinforce what they already know as well as realize they know more than they thought they did.

2. Have students ask children in their field placement schools to look at a new piece of software and discuss what they know about it from other software they've seen. Students guide them toward identifying the following similarities across different word processing programs:

    •   File management activities, such as: Start New, Open a Saved File, Save a File, Print, Rename, Quit
    •   Editing activities, such as: Cut, Paste, Copy, Font Selection, Type Alignment, Line Spacing
    •   Spell check, thesaurus, and grammar capabilities
    •   Chart or table creation, formula input, and graphing

5B. LEARNED HELPLESSNESS

While boys are often encouraged to investigate possible approaches to problems and obstacles, teachers, who do not realize they hold different expectations and treat children differently by gender, often finish tasks for girls who hit a road block. This is one of the ways in which girls learn to believe they are not capable of finding solutions or solving problems on their own. Girls need to have experiences with developing their own autonomous problem-solving abilities or they will have difficulty becoming independent learners and capable adult workers. Preservice teachers need to realize that "doing it for the girls" instead of coaching them to do it for themselves does them no favors.

ACTIVITY 161. LITERATURE ON LEARNED HELPLESSNESS   OUT OF CLASS / IN CLASS

1. Invite your students to read about learned helplessness:

    *   Peter Kloosterman, "Academic Learned Helplessness, Mastery Orientation, Motivation, and Achievement." (See Volume II, Resources. This section is on pp. 104-107.)

2. In class, invite students to cite instances where they may have been taught that they were not competent in a given area. Ask how their treatment compared to that which their brothers and sisters received. Discuss the implications for teaching behaviors.

ACTIVITY 162. CLASSROOM OBSERVATIONS   FIELD / IN CLASS

1. Have students observe field placement classes at times when children are working on their own, either at their desks, in groups, or in lab settings. Ask them to observe the teacher's behavior each time a child asks for help. Does the teacher provide a clue or a suggestion and leave the child to solve the problem alone? Or does the teacher give the child the answer or even pick up the pencil and write the answer (or type it on the keyboard) for the child? Have students write down each incident: what happened and whether the child was male or female.

2. In class, discuss your students' observation results.

ACTIVITY 163. VIGNETTE: DANIEL AND SUSAN IN CLASS

1. Ask students to read the following vignette, found in Volume II on page 67.

    David and Susan are each working on focusing microscopes in tenth grade biology lab. Their lab stations are adjacent to each other. Susan is frustrated: She just cannot get the microscope to focus. David is having difficulty as well. They call the teacher, Mr. Bauer, over for assistance.

    Mr. Bauer looks into Susan's microscope and focuses the image for her. "Thanks!" says Susan. Mr. Bauer then looks into David's microscope and says to him, "Just turn the fine adjustment slightly and you should get it focused." David works on it by himself.

    What might Susan be thinking? What do you think David is thinking? Which student received the best help? Why? How is this related to learned helplessness?

2. Ask students to discuss it in small groups.

ACTIVITY 164. OUR THROWAWAY SOCIETY YOUR TIME / IN CLASS

> *Note: this activity works best when at least one-third of the students are male. If you don't have enough males in your class, you may be able to "borrow" some.*

1. Collect used small appliances such as hair dryers, electric knives, popcorn poppers, toasters, coffee grinders, blenders, and so forth, at garage sales. They don't even have to work. Remove the plugs for safety.

2. Borrow or supply a collection of basic tools: screwdrivers (lots of Phillips and some slotted), pliers (several needle-nose and some regular), wrenches (allen and regular), hammers, mallets, chisels, awls, tweezers, magnifying glasses, and so on. Students will primarily need Phillips screwdrivers and needle-nose pliers.

3. Organize the students in groups of two, mixing the sexes whenever possible. Distribute one appliance per pair or let pairs choose, and then give them the following directions:

    a. Dismantle the appliance.
    b. Prepare a written and/or drawn description of the inside of the appliance. How many pieces can you remove and replace? How are they organized?
    c. Reassemble the appliance.

4. Preferably videotape the groups as they work, or have someone on the sidelines taking notes about how the groups are working. Who does the recording? Who proposes things to try? Who makes the decisions? Who chooses and handles the tools? Who explains what to whom?

5. Optional: Circulate as groups work, purposely doing some things that favor males and encourage learned helplessness among females, such as:

- Taking tools from female students and giving them to males
- Asking male students many questions and giving them a lot of wait time for answers
- Tell female students how to do things instead of waiting for their ideas
- Encourage groups to compete: Which group can dismantle its appliance and return it to its original state first?

6. Post-lab discussion: Ask students about their group interactions using the questions in Step 4. If you have a video of their work, show it now for analysis. If there were gender-biased interactions, did students realize it at the time? If so, how did they feel? What are the implications for the children in their future classrooms?

ACTIVITY 165. ROLE PLAY   **IN CLASS**

1. Have your students role-play children in a class and a teacher who carries out tasks, solves problems, or answers questions for female students but not male students, without realizing what she or he is doing.

2. Ask your students to discuss how they felt during the role play.

3. Ask students to summarize orally or in writing the effect of learned helplessness on performance for the female learner.

ACTIVITY 166. DEMYSTIFYING THE COMPUTER   **IN CLASS**
                                                                              TECHNOLOGY

1. Explain to your students that girls are often not encouraged to explore and inspect equipment in the same ways as boys.

2. Contact a computer service in your area or put a classified ad in the local paper to obtain the donation of an old PC or Mac that can be taken apart.

3. Having your students do the hands-on work, find the following components and discuss their purpose:

- Motherboard
- SIMMS memory
- ROM chip
- Disk drive
- Hard drive

- Fan
- Speaker
- Mouse card
- Expansion slots

ACTIVITY 167. INTERVIEW NEIGHBORS AND/OR TEENAGERS   OUT OF CLASS / IN CLASS

1. Ask students to interview four to six adult neighbors, half men and half women. The activity can be done with teenagers instead of, or in addition to, adults. Ask them to use the following questions:

    - Do you have a VCR? If so, do you know how to program it?
    - Do you have a stereo? If so, who hooked it up?
    - Do you have a microwave oven? If so, can you use all the features (including defrost, warm, cook, etc.)?
    - Do you have a computer? Who set it up? What do you do when it doesn't work?

2. Ask students to write up and share their findings.

3. In a class discussion, ask students if they found any gender patterns in their combined interviews. How will this information influence their teaching?

5C. RISK-TAKING BEHAVIOR

Mathematics, science, and technology are learned best when students are encouraged to construct their own knowledge, which requires taking risks, trial and error, and learning from mistakes. This type of behavior is often not fostered in females, who can feel incompetent when they do not get the correct answer immediately. Preservice teachers need to develop a repertoire of instructional techniques that create situations where females can construct knowledge, take risks, tolerate ambiguity, and investigate solutions in order to develop an understanding and appreciation for MST.

ACTIVITY 168. THE EARLY YEARS   OUT OF CLASS / IN CLASS

1. Ask students to read Selma Greenberg's work on early childhood school environments. Emphasize her point that what girls need most from kindergarten is considered optional: recess activities, large motor skills, and building in the block corner, while what boys need most from kindergarten is required: following rules, listening to peers and teachers, and improving communication skills.

    •   Greenberg, Selma (1985). "Equity in Early Childhood Environments" in *The Handbook for Achieving Sex Equity Through Education*.

    •   Greenberg, Selma (1978). *Right From the Start: A Guide to Nonsexist Child Rearing*.

2. Have students discuss this material in class. Identify the relation of typical "boy behavior" at early ages to a willingness to take risks in science, math, or technology. Examples are block building, knocking down and re-building, flying model planes, racing cars, and so forth.

ACTIVITY 169. AUTONOMOUS LEARNING BEHAVIORS   OUT OF CLASS / IN CLASS

1. Ask students to refer to:

    •   The schematic of Elizabeth Fennema's "Autonomous Learning Behavior Model," page 68, Volume II).

2. Have students research and define behaviors such as working independently, performing high cognitive tasks, and so on. A recommended resource is:

    •   Meyer, Margaret R. and Koehler, Mary S. (1990). "Internal Influences on Gender Differences in Mathematics" in *Mathematics and Gender*.

3. Discuss how internal motivational beliefs and societal influences affect the development of autonomous learning behaviors.

ACTIVITY 170. CONSTRUCTION OF KNOWLEDGE   **IN CLASS**

MATHEMATICS

1. Present the following geometry example to your students:

   Draw at least three different rectangles with areas of 24 sq. cm. Is the perimeter always the same? Explain your answer.

2. Distribute graph paper and have them work in groups on the example.

3. At the conclusion of the exercise, ask them to write about what they have learned about perimeter and area.

4. Discuss with students the understanding gained by constructing knowledge as opposed to learning formulas, and how they think girls and boys would relate to this exercise.

ACTIVITY 171. DEVELOPING A SENSE OF COMPETENCE IN FEMALES   **IN CLASS / FIELD**

1. Ask students to consider the following classroom strategies:

   - Cooperative learning groups
   - Student-selected topics for projects
   - Class discussions
   - Experiential learning, such as field trips
   - Student evaluations of each other's work

2. Discuss how each point can help females develop a sense of competence and independence when doing mathematics, science, or technology.

3. Have students test each strategy by working in a classroom on creating student-centered activities.

5D. SOCIAL PRESSURES

Social pressures on children to behave in stereotyped sex-role ways increase drastically as they enter adolescence. Research shows that girls' self-esteem drops dramatically as they enter the upper grades and social issues take priority over academic ones. Because girls think they will be unpopular if they are perceived as brainy or if they perform better than boys in MST, many succumb to the pressure to be "feminine," which means not being too smart and not being too good at "boy stuff" — science, math, and technology. The conflicts are further complicated for women from cultures where MST are considered unnecessary or even unfeminine for girls. Preservice teachers need to learn techniques that support a learning environment where learning MST is a positive experience for girls and where their success is respected.

ACTIVITY 172. SOCIAL PRESSURES AND BEHAVIOR   IN CLASS

1. Ask students to write a list of adjectives they think describe a typical seventh grade boy and a typical seventh grade girl (or choose another grade they can relate to better).

2. Have students read their lists and generate a class list of characteristics that were mentioned most often for girls and boys.

3. Compare the traits and discuss how the descriptions reflect social pressures and how they affect MST learning in the classroom.

ACTIVITY 173. WHAT DO THE KIDS THINK?   FIELD

1. Ask students to develop an instrument to explore what children feel about particular attributes of the opposite gender, and of their own gender. For example, they can ask children to rank qualities for each gender separately in order of most important to least important:

    *   Good looking
    *   Intelligent
    *   Sexy
    *   Friendly
    *   Quiet

    *   Athletic
    *   Flexible
    *   Organized
    *   Studious
    *   Fun

2. Ask students to report their findings to the class. What do their students believe are the most important qualities in a boy? In a girl?

ACTIVITY 174. INTERVIEWS   OUT OF CLASS / IN CLASS

1. Have students interview women working in mathematics, science, or technology to learn about the social pressures they felt while pursuing a career and how they dealt with the pressures.

2. In a class discussion, students should explore common experiences among the women interviewed. For example,

    *   Did the women feel isolated in high school courses?
    *   Did the women feel isolated in college courses?
    *   Did teachers and professors treat them differently from males? How?
    *   What strategies did the women devise to deal with the pressures?

ACTIVITY 175. GROUP PROJECTS   IN CLASS / OUT OF CLASS

1. Assign groups of students the following question:

    What strategies and techniques can be used to create a supportive environment that develops confidence, builds self-esteem, and encourages respect for female students?

2. Groups work together to research techniques and strategies recommended to teach mathematics equitably and should be as specific as possible in their response. Recommended resources:

    *   Sanders, Jo (1994). *Lifting the Barriers: 600 Strategies That Really Work to Increase Girls' Participation in Science, Mathematics and Computers.*

    *   National Coalition of Girls' Schools (1992). *Math and Science for Girls, A Symposium.*

    *   Clewell, Beatriz Chu, et al. (1992). *Breaking the Barriers: Helping Female and Minority Students Succeed in Mathematics and Science.*

    *   Davis, Cinda-Sue & Rosser, Sue (1996). "Program and curricular interventions" in *The Equity Equation: Fostering the Advancement of Women in the Sciences, Mathematics and Engineering.*

3. Groups present their findings to the class.

ACTIVITY 176. VIGNETTE: THE AV SQUAD   IN CLASS

1. Ask students to refer to the following vignette, found on page 69 in Volume II.

In your school, the A-V squad, which handles all the technology equipment including the TV, the VCR, and the laser video-disk player, is all male. You suggest to several girls in your class that they consider joining the squad.

"Oh, no," says Lakeesha, "that's just for boys." Lila agrees: "Girls don't know how to do those mechanical things. I sure don't!" "The boys would never let me touch that stuff!" chimes in Sarita.

What is the effect of these beliefs on girls? What would you do about this situation?

2.   Ask students to discuss it in small groups.

ACTIVITY 177. GETTING MESSY   **IN CLASS / OUT OF CLASS**

                                                                 SCIENCE

1.   Ask students to read "Tips for Teachers," pages 70-78 in Volume II.

2.   Ask them to discuss the social pressures on girls not to get messy ("It's icky! It's yukky! It's disgusting!") and what this implies for science learning.

3.   Ask them to write a lesson plan describing a "getting messy" science lesson and strategies they would employ to involve girls as much as possible.

EQUITY ISSUE 6

TESTING AND ASSESSMENT

Traditional forms of testing can place girls at a disadvantage when methods and content capitalize on skills boys are more likely to have than girls. We know that females are better course takers than they are test takers. Gender differences in achievement may be the result of the testing process and not an indication of girls' lesser abilities. They moreover perpetuate stereotypes of girls' "deficient" achievement in mathematics, science, and technology. The recent advent of performance assessment and more authentic measurements for assessing what students know in real-life contexts is consonant with what works best for girls and young women.

6A. TEST DESIGN FAVORS MALES

Girls have historically scored lower on mathematics, science, and technology achievement tests than do boys. This may be due to bias in testing methods, not to ability. Girls are less likely to take a risk and guess at multiple-choice questions than are boys. They do less well in competitive timed test situations and when tests require decontextualized bits of information that have been memorized. Another issue is the way test results are reported, including the bell curve. Exposing preservice teachers to what we know about girls and testing and alternative modes of assessment will help encourage girls' achievement in science.

ACTIVITY 178. RESEARCH ON BIAS IN TESTING　　　　　　　　　　　　**OUT OF CLASS / IN CLASS**

1. Assign the following readings to students:

    - "Sex and Gender Bias in Testing" in AAUW Foundation. (1992) *How Schools Shortchange Girls*, pages 52-57. In the 1995 Marlowe edition, see pp. 89-99.
    - Linn, Marcia (1992). "Gender Differences in Educational Achievement" in *Sex Equity in Educational Opportunity, Achievement, and Testing.* Proceedings of the 1991 Invitational Conference of the Educational Testing Service, Princeton, NJ, 1992.

2. Remind students that both the new mathematics standards and the science standards call for equal assessment of learning achievement.

3. In class, ask students to generate recommendations for alternative methods of assessment that will more accurately reflect girls' skills and abilities. The list of recommendations should include:

- Offering a range of modalities for assessment
- Assessing integrated understanding
- The use of writing vehicles to assess science understandings
- Employing performance tasks to measure ability with science process skills

ACTIVITY 179. MULTIPLE-CHOICE TEST PERFORMANCE RESULTS   OUT OF CLASS

1. Have students obtain data on mathematics and science performance from the National Assessment of Educational Progress (NAEP) over the past three years.

2. They record achievement results for males and females on the most recent NAEP assessments for multiple-choice items and open-ended problems.

3. They compare recent results with earlier ones and make generalizations regarding gender performance on multiple-choice tests and open-ended items.

ACTIVITY 180. TEST-TAKING TECHNIQUES   IN CLASS / OUT OF CLASS

1. Administer an elementary or secondary level mathematics or science standardized test to your students. Practice tests can be obtained from local school districts and/or test publishers.

2. When completed, discuss techniques students used to take the test (i.e., guessing, estimating, eliminating unreasonable answers).

3. Use published practice materials (such as Steck-Vaughn or Curriculum Associates: See Volume II, Resources) to find examples of test items that can be used to model and teach each test-taking technique.

4. Relate these skills to gender equity by referring students to:

- Clewell, Beatriz Chu et al. (1992). *Breaking the Barriers: Helping Female and Minority Students Succeed in Mathematics and Science*, pages 77-78.

5. Ask students to write a lesson plan to teach test-taking techniques to female (and male) students.

ACTIVITY 181. OTHER FORMS OF ASSESSMENT   **IN CLASS / FIELD**

1. In class, list and define alternative formats used in assessment including: cooperative testing, untimed tests, extended-time tests, take-home exams, oral exams, performance assessment, portfolio assessment, and open-ended assessment.

2. Students can obtain samples of these types of assessment from current literature. See the listings under Assessment Resources in Volume II. Also examine:

   - *Math Assessment, Myths, Models and Practices*, NCTM
   - *Assessment Alternatives in Mathematics*, EQUALS
   - *Science Assessment in Service of Reform* by Shirley Malcom and Gerlad Kulm
   - *Active Assessment for Active Science* by George Hein
   - *National Science Education Standards* by The National Research Council

3. Assign groups or pairs of students to research and report on the use and validity of alternative forms of assessment and its effect on the female learner, each group looking into a different form.

4. Have your students administer a test using one of the modifications or an alternative form of assessment to a class of elementary or secondary school students and analyze the results for males and females.

ACTIVITY 182. NCTM ASSESSMENT STANDARDS   **OUT OF CLASS**

                                                              MATHEMATICS

1. Provide a copy of Standard 3, *Assessment Standards*, from National Council of Teachers of Mathematics (NCTM).

2. Ask students to read and write a summary on the Equity Standard.

ACTIVITY 183. NATIONAL SCIENCE ASSESSMENT STANDARDS   **OUT OF CLASS**

                                                                      SCIENCE

1. Ask students to read chapter 5 of the National Science Education Standards (National Research Council, 1995), noting especially Standard B, "Assessing the Opportunity to Learn Science."

2. Have them write a page on the gender implications of this standard.

ACTIVITY 184. NEW TRENDS IN ASSESSMENT   **IN CLASS / OUT OF CLASS**

1. Ask students to gather information and/or samples of nonsecure alternative assessment from state and city boards of education. For suggestions, see Assessment Resources in Volume II.

2. Refer students to "Assessment Profile," page 79 in Volume II, that calls for them to complete the following information on the assessment program they study:

   - Name of assessment
   - State/city
   - Year began
   - Grades administered
   - Type of assessment
   - How the assessment addresses the relevant education standard

3. This information can be filed in a database to be added to during the course and used for future reference.

ACTIVITY 185. CHILD-GENERATED ASSESSMENT   **FIELD**

1. After your students teach a lesson in their field placement class, have them ask the children which particular activity from the lesson was their favorite, and why.

2. Ask students to draw conclusions based on children's answers, their sex, and what they felt the answers indicated about what the children had learned from the activities they preferred. They should also consider what they themselves learned about the effectiveness of their own teaching.

3. Have students write an assessment based on children's answers.

ACTIVITY 186. WRITING AND SCIENCE   **IN CLASS / FIELD**
                                                         SCIENCE

1. Ask students to examine ways in which writing may be used to assess students in science. A laboratory research notebook and new ways to write up lab reports encourage greater creativity and allow for fuller expression.

2. Ask students to refer to "Writing Prompts" on pages 80-81 of Volume II.

3. Ask students to try out one writing assignment in science in their field placement. They should report the results back to class.

6B. TEST ITEMS FAVOR MALE INTERESTS

Research has shown that boys tend to do better than girls with test items whose content and context favor male interests, refer less to women, or present women in stereotypical roles. Girls tend to have more success with real-life application problems in mathematics, science, and technology, and with process skill questions than straight content questions. When test content does not reflect girls' knowledge and strengths, their scores are artificially low.

ACTIVITY 187. STANDARDIZED TEST QUESTIONS   **OUT OF CLASS**

1. Have standardized tests available for your students to examine. See Volume II, Resources, for assessment resources.

2. Ask students to examine each test item in terms of context, gender, and type of knowledge:

    •   The context of the specific question: Is it gender related?
    •   The gender of the people described in a given question.
    •   The type of knowledge that is being accessed: Is it recall or deeper understanding? Deeper understanding questions do not ask for isolated bits of knowledge.

ACTIVITY 188. PERFORMANCE ASSESSMENT TASKS   **OUT OF CLASS / FIELD / IN CLASS**

1. Ask students to choose a science or mathematics concept and devise a performance assessment task for students to demonstrate their understanding of the concept. Compile these assessment tasks into a class book, available to each student for future use.

2. For the same concept, ask students next to develop a multiple-choice test. Ask them to compare the two methods and evaluate what can be learned about students' understanding of the concept from each method.

3. Invite students to try out their performance assessment tasks with students in their field placement, and to report back to the class on how the performance tasks were received by the girls. If they choose, they can also administer the multiple-choice version, and compare students' performance and reactions.

4. Ask students to read "Assessment, Authenticity, Context, and Validity" by Grant Wiggins (see Volume II, Resources). Discuss in class: In what ways is authentic assessment a more "female-friendly" approach to assessment? Discuss the role of context in various forms of assessments.

ACTIVITY 189. EVALUATING THE PERFORMANCE TASK   IN CLASS

1. There is little research on performance testing and gender bias. However, there is some indication that there may be gender bias on the part of some observers who expect girls to perform the task less well than boys.

2. Ask students to establish a list of criteria for judging a child's performance in one of their tasks in the preceding activity.

3. Brainstorm ways in which the observer could be gender-biased in evaluating the performance on this task, and ways to prevent such bias from occuring.

ACTIVITY 190. BIAS IN TESTS   OUT OF CLASS

1. Ask students to design a checklist that would be appropriate to use for evaluating bias in test items.

2. Have them obtain copies of nonsecure multiple-choice tests by contacting test companies or publishers of test practice materials.

3. Using the checklist they have designed, students evaluate these tests for biased items.

ACTIVITY 191. THE EQUITY PRINCIPLE   OUT OF CLASS
                                                      MATHEMATICS

1. Assign pages 129-131 in *Measuring What Counts* (Mathematical Sciences Education Board, 1993; see Resources, Volume II), and define the "Equity Principle" for mathematics assessments.

2. Ask students to prepare a written report concerning gender equity about the impact of multiple-choice, timed tests on female learners in terms of:

   • Fairness and comparability
   • Opportunity to learn
   • Access

ACTIVITY 192. CREATING AN UNBIASED TEST   OUT OF CLASS

1. Have students contact major test publishers (such as CTB-McGraw/Hill, Psychological Corporation, Riverside) for information on how test content is evaluated for bias. See Volume II for phone numbers.

2. They use the information to create a nonbiased test that is appropriate for grade and content level using multiple forms of assessment.

PART 3

ASSESSING YOUR STUDENTS' GENDER EQUITY LEARNING

In this section we provide sample measures of student change written by Patricia B. Campbell, PhD (Campbell-Kibler Associates, Inc., Groton Ridge Heights, Groton MA 01450, (508) 448-5402), <ckassoc@tiac.net>, for the participants in the Teacher Education Equity Project. They can be used at the beginning and end of your course as pre-/post measures, or you may want to use them instead as teaching activities.

INDIVIDUAL SCENARIOS

These can be used at the beginning and end of teacher education courses as pre-/ post measures

Elementary Methods Courses

1. You have been observing what choices students make in your early childhood classroom and have discovered that during free time lots of boys and almost no girls are running around and playing informal sports games, while lots of girls and almost no boys are playing board games. What, if anything, do you do? Why did you decide to respond in this way?

2. Your class is working with owl pellets but Angela, Anthony and Jennifer don't want to do it because it is "yucky." What do you do? Justify your response.

3. In a class discussion, most of the girls as well as the boys agree that boys are better than girls in the subject you teach. What, if anything, do you do? Justify your response.

4. In the computer center you notice that Jennifer, the assigned keyboarder, has been pushed away by the more aggressive Todd. What, if anything, do you do? Justify your response.

Secondary Methods Courses

1. You are dissecting fetal pigs with your class, but Angela, Anthony and Jennifer don't want to do it because it is "gross." What do you do? Justify your response.

2. In the physics lab you notice that Jennifer, the assigned group leader, has been co-opted by the more aggressive Todd. What, if anything, do you do? Justify your response.

Elementary and Secondary Methods Courses

1. After checking your own behavior, you discover that students are getting different amounts and types of attention from you based on their gender and race. In general boys are getting more positive and negative attention from you than are girls, with African-American boys getting the most negative attention. What, if anything, do you do? Why did you decide to respond in this way?

2. You are using cooperative learning in your class and you notice that while Susie, Kiesha and Joan are involved, they don't seem to be participating in activities that call for using tools or other hands-on materials. What, if anything, do you do? Why did you decide to respond in this way?

3. In a parent conference, Doreen's parents say it really isn't that important for Doreen to do well in math. After all, Louella, Doreen's mother, has always hated math and it never negatively affected her life. What, if anything do you do? Why did you decide to respond in this way?

4. All of the parental assistance that you get is from mothers. What, if anything do you do? Why?

CLASS-UNIT MALE/FEMALE SCENARIOS

These questions can be asked pre/post or post only. Either way, half the students should get the scenario with the boy's name, while the other half should get the scenario with the girl's name.

Elementary Methods Courses

1. The Aggressive Child

    You have been student teaching for several weeks and during this time one student, Stella, has been acting very aggressively toward the other children. While you are in charge of the class Stella picks up a block and deliberately throws it at you, hitting you in the leg (it hurts!). What do you do?

    You have been student teaching for several weeks and during this time one student, Steven, has been acting very aggressively toward the other children. While you are in charge of the class Steven picks up a block and deliberately throws it at you, hitting you in the leg (it hurts!). What do you do?

2. The Passive Child

    For the past week Maria has been withdrawn, not speaking up in class and not playing very much with the other children at recess. You have asked what is wrong and she says nothing, but she follows you around whenever she can. What do you do?

    For the past week Jose has been withdrawn, not speaking up in class and not playing very much with the other children at recess. You have asked what is wrong and he says nothing, but he follows you around whenever he can. What do you do?

Elementary and Secondary Methods Courses

Providing Help

> Adrienne is not the best math student in the world but she does try. She has been working on a problem on dividing by fractions (What is 1/2 divided by 1/4?) for what seems like forever and has come to you for help. Describe what, if anything, you do to help her.

> Mason is not the best math student in the world but he does try. He has been working on a problem on dividing by fractions (What is 1/2 divided by 1/4?) for what seems like forever and has come to you for help. Describe what, if anything, you do to help him.

ESSAY QUESTIONS

1. You are interested in finding out who participates the most in your classroom and who doesn't and if there are any patterns by gender and by race. List two different ways you could find this out.

2. What kinds of things can teachers do to encourage all students, girls as well as boys, to become more interested in and involved with math, science, and/or technology?

3. What is gender equity? List some strategies teachers can use to achieve gender equity in their classes.

Your analysis of students' answers can include:

- The number and variety of strategies listed

- The quality of the strategies in terms of their:
  — Potential for effectiveness
  — Sensitivity to gender and race issues
  — Consistency of educational philosophy

- The quality of the student's rationale including:
  — The use of research
  — The degree to which potential negative and positive results have been thought out

- At the class level, similarities and differences in response to the same scenario with female/male variations

PART 4

ACTION RESEARCH PROJECTS

Many of the activities in Part 1 of this book can be used by students as action research projects in three ways: either as individual efforts or group efforts in which everyone does the same thing and compares results or people do smaller parts of one thing and fit the parts together at the end. We have seen the value of this hands-on, constructivist approach to learning many times over, and warmly urge you to adopt the approach as much as is feasible with your students.

EVALUATION SOURCE MATERIALS FOR YOUR STUDENTS

First, we would like to refer you to several source materials for your students in Volume II that were written by Patricia B. Campbell for the Teacher Education Equity Project participants. We hope they will be of help to you as you guide your students in conducting their action research projects.

- A Beginner's Guide to Educational Research, pages 82-84

- Materials on evaluating action research projects:

    Evaluation and Documentation, or Why Should I Do This? Page 85
    Can Evaluation Be Useful and Even Fun? Page 86

- Materials your students can use to assess gender-related attitudes and behavior by:

    Sample Gender Attitude Survey Questions, pages 87-88
    Sample Gender Behavior Survey Questions, pages 89-90

- Materials your students (or you) can use to evaluate workshops for inservice or preservice teachers

    Workshop Program Evaluation, page 91
    Workshop Follow-up Form, page 92

TEACHER EDUCATION EQUITY PROJECT PARTICIPANTS' MINI-GRANT PROJECTS

The Teacher Education Equity Project made available to each participant a small mini-grant ($750 per person) to carry out a project that met four criteria:

1. It concerned <u>pre</u>service education
2. It concerned gender equity
3. It concerned mathematics, science, and/or technology
4. It actively involved the preservice students

To give you some ideas of the types of projects your students could carry out, we present the projects carried out by the participants of the Teacher Education Equity Project. In most cases, the amount of the mini-grant they received from the project could either be replaced by departmental or college funds, raised privately, or dispensed with entirely. If you would like more information, their names and addresses, correct as of 1996, can be found at the end of the project summaries.

ALASKA.   Rusty Myers, Alaska Pacific University —

To have preservice students prepare a newsletter on gender equity to be distributed to teachers statewide in this largely rural state, and with students' help to create and circulate three kits of gender equity materials to teachers statewide.

ARKANSAS.   Rose Steelman, University of Central Arkansas —

To have preservice students review texts for bias, survey elementary teachers for gender attitudes, collect biased and gender-fair articles and photos, and present findings to students, faculty and in-service teachers; to observe selected students in directed teaching, give them a seminar in gender equity, observe them again, and present results of pre-/post observations; and to incorporate a three-part gender equity seminar as a permanent part of the direct teaching experience.

FLORIDA.   George O'Brien, Yee-Ping Soon, Florida International University —

To have preservice students select gender equity materials in mathematics and science; to analyze the gender equity components of the dynamics of different groupings of students using Lego Logo; and to have preservice students conduct a series of workshops for in-service teachers on gender equity.

GEORGIA.   Cherry Brewton, Georgia Southern University —

To have early childhood education majors conduct a workshop on gender equity for new early childhood practicum preservice teachers.

HAWAII.   Joe Zilliox, Frank Walton, University of Hawaii —

To determine the use levels and impact of a collection of materials on gender equity in education to be used by preservice students, university faculty, and in-service teachers.

IDAHO.   Gwen Kelly, University of Idaho —

To have preservice students investigate several research questions: whether girls and boys respond differently to specific lessons, what content/cognitive lesson modifications hold girls' vs. boys' interest most, what management/delivery modifications hold girls' vs. boys' interest most, and what lesson modifications can be made to promote equity fairness in mixed-sex classrooms. Students collect data by teaching and observing in junior high classrooms.

— Rickie Miller, Jenny Piazza, Susan Chevelier, Boise State University —

To have preservice students interview children for gender beliefs, analyze children's literature and software for gender bias, and help teach a day-long retreat for College of Education faculty on gender equity in education.

INDIANA.   Jerry Krockover, Dan Shepardson, Purdue University —

To have preservice students carry out quantitative and qualitative classroom observations in an elementary school, present their findings to the school's faculty, and write an article for the Journal of Science Teacher Education.

— Rick Breault, Marie Theobald, University of Indianapolis —

To have preservice students participate in the planning and the giving of a three-session workshop for 10 middle-school teachers of math, science and computer classes (March, information and awareness; April or May, action planning; early fall, update and evaluation)   A few students also speak to female middle-school students and others evaluate the middle-school teachers' action plans.

IOWA. Martha Voyles, Grinnell College —

To train six preservice students who are strong in math or science to attend some classes with and serve as mentors and "encouragers" for six high school girls who seem to be falling out of the math pipeline in Algebra I.

KANSAS. Barbara Attivo, Twyla Sherman, Cathy Yeotis, Wichita State University —

To conduct an Expanding Your Horizons conference for 300 middle-school girls, 30 science and math teachers, and 45 parents, on careers in math, science and technology for women.   Preservice students help to teach the conference.

KENTUCKY. Robert Boram, Joyce Saxon, Morehead State University —

To have about 100 preservice students, working in groups with six faculty members, develop action research projects to determine which teaching strategies are most effective in increasing children's awareness of career opportunities for women in science, mathematics, and technology.

— Kathi Matthew, Alice Mikovch, Western Kentucky University —

To train preservice students about biased classroom interaction patterns, have them code university faculty, hold a gender equity workshop for university faculty, re-code university faculty, analyze data from first and second codings, and present findings to university faculty.

— Max Hines, University of Louisville —

To have preservice students design and carry out a research project to determine gender equity understanding among math, science, and technology teachers at five to 10 area high schools. She will compare the classroom equity behavior of participating students to those who receive gender equity instruction but don't take part in the research project.

— Karen Karp, University of Louisville —

To integrate a component on children's literature with female protagonists into the elementary math methods course.

MICHIGAN.   Shirley Freed, Andrews University —

To have elementary math methods students observe verbal interaction patterns in K-8 classrooms, interview K-8 math students, videotape and analyze interaction patterns in K-8 classrooms, and facilitate math study teams after school especially for girls.

— Ray Ostrander, Andrews University —

To have four preservice students create a list of gender-biased behaviors from the research, observe in a nearby high school computer technology classroom, and report their results at a meeting of an organization of undergraduate education students.

— John Novak, Dave Johnson, Eastern Michigan University —

To have preservice students research and produce biographies of local women in math and science careers, with questions and hands-on activities, in elementary and secondary versions, to be used by the students in their field placement schools.

MISSISSIPPI.   Pamela Freeman, Mississippi State University —

To have preservice students teach a workshop on gender equity to parents.

MISSOURI.   Pat Lucido, Northwest Missouri State University —

To have preservice students analyze classroom interaction patterns using and comparing results from two methods: Newton Message Pads with Sunburst's Learning Profile software, and the pencil-and-paper Shepardson-Pizzini form. Students' observations of video clips of classroom lessons will also be compared pre- and post-gender equity instruction.

MONTANA.   Korinne Tande, Montana State University/Northern —

To hold an overnight camp on math, science, and technology for 20 Native American girls entering 6th grade, located on the university campus and directed by preservice students.

— Elisabeth Charron, Montana State University/Bozeman —

To hold a three-day conference for 30 cooperating teachers statewide (lead teachers and mentor teachers) and outstanding preservice teachers, with followup throughout the remaining school year, with the active participation of preservice students.

NEW JERSEY.   Frank Curriero, Jersey City State College —

To have preservice students analyze children's books involving science and/or math for elementary students, and to distribute the printed analysis to local schools and New Jersey math and science teachers associations for publication.

NEW MEXICO. Donna Gee, Aurora Hodgden, Eastern New Mexico University —

To have preservice students and faculty present an in-service workshop on gender equity in elementary science and mathematics, highlighting the use of children's literature in these areas.

NEW YORK. Brenda Peters, Huey Bogan, Maureen Gillette, College of St. Rose —

To have preservice students in math and science design and carry out action research projects in their field experience schools for course credit, and to have them create a multi-media presentation on their findings for teachers, administrators, and others.

— Sheila Smith-Hobson, Lehman College —

To have preservice students evaluate educational software with respect to gender equity and give a presentation to other preservice students on what they learn.

NORTH CAROLINA. Leah McCoy, Wake Forest University —

To have preservice students research the lives and contributions of women mathematicians, work with students in the Communications Department to prepare a script, props, and so on, choose student actors to portray the mathematicians, and create a 30-minute tape on five to seven figures. Students help teach a workshop to teachers at the "premiere" of the tape, to be used in local schools.

— Barb Levin, Kathy Matthews, University of North Carolina/Greensboro —

To develop, test and disseminate a hypercard stack on gender equity to be used by students as an alternative instructional vehicle.

OHIO. Mike Grote, Ohio Wesleyan —

To team elementary math and science preservice students with upper-class female math and science majors. Pairs construct hands-on math and science exhibits and present them to middle-school children.

— Mike Beeth, Ohio State University —

To involve preservice students in the planning and teaching of an existing week-long summer camp program on math, science, and computers for 150 seventh- and eighth-grade girls called BE WISE.

OREGON. Maggie Niess, Karen Higgins, Oregon State University —

To have recently graduated MAT preservice students plan and present a conference on gender equity to new MAT students.

PENNSYLVANIA. Tom Lord, Meghan Twiest, Margaret Stempien, Indiana Univ. of Pennsylvania —

To enlist preservice students in observations on gender equity in field experience schools in a research project format; to hold a day-long seminar for faculty at several nearby universities.

SOUTH DAKOTA.   Mike Cass, Dorothy Spethmann, Dakota State University —

To train supervising teachers in gender equity and to have preservice teachers teach their cooperating teachers about gender equity.

UTAH.   Shirley Leali, Weber State University —

To hold a one-day workshop for 15 elementary Teacher Leaders with the assistance of eight preservice students; have the Teacher Leaders teach cooperating teachers about gender equity, collect classroom data, and review texts; and have preservice students choose the Teacher Leader who writes the best one-page proposal on how she or he would use $50 in project funds for gender equity materials in the classroom.

VERMONT.   Jody Kenny, St. Michael's College —

To prepare the May '96 issue of the *New England Mathematics Journal* on the theme of gender equity, with articles by students if possible, Teacher Education Equity Project participants, and others, with copies distributed to all participants.

— Joyce Morris, Charlie Rathbone, Clint Erb, University of Vermont —

To have preservice students participate in conducting a conference on gender equity for 50 students, faculty and local teachers.

WEST VIRGINIA. Judy Werner, West Virginia University —

To compare the classroom interaction behaviors with respect to gender equity in field placement settings of a group of preservice mathematics teachers who have been exposed to gender equity instruction in class with another group who have not. The preservice students will present the results of this study to their classmates.

WISCONSIN.   Patsy Brooks, Alverno College —

To create a Technology Scholars program at this women's college: to enlist female students with computer skills to assist faculty to plan and implement gender-equitable instruction involving computers.

— Ken Welty, University of Wisconsin/Stout —

To have preservice teachers develop gender-fair learning activities for, in, and with elementary technology classes, in part using manipulatives for hands-on learning, and to develop a monograph of the activities to be disseminated to technology teachers in Wisconsin via the Wisconsin Department of Public Instruction and the Wisconsin Technology Education Association.

— Sandy Madison, University of Wisconsin/Stevens Point —

To have preservice students plan and participate in the Central Wisconsin Computer Education Conference for methods students, K-12 teachers and administrators, and post-secondary computer science educators. The focus of the conference is gender equity; the title is general to avoid attracting only the converted.

TEACHER EDUCATION EQUITY PROJECT PARTICIPANTS

CORRECT AS OF 1997

U.S.	NAME	ADDRESS	PHONE & FAX	E-MAIL
	Sanders, Jo Project Director	Washington Research Institute 150 Nickerson St., Suite 305 Seattle, WA 98109	(206) 285-9317 F 285-1523	jsanders@halcyon.com
AK	Myers, Richard	Alaska Pacific University 4101 University Drive Anchorage AK 99508	907-564-8257 F 562-4276	
AR	Steelman, Rose	University of Central Arkansas Box 4913 201 Donaghey Conway AR 72035	501-450-5456 F 450-5468	roses@cc1.uca.edu
CO	Chevalier, Susan	Adams State College Teacher Education College E. S. 230 Alamosa CO 81102	719-589-7331	
CO	Leali, Shirley	University of Nothern Colorado School for the Study of Teaching and Teacher Education Greeley CO 80639	970-351-2005 F 304-1368	saleali@bentley. univnorthco.edu
CO	Piazza, Jenny	University of Southern Colorado Ctr. for Learning, Teaching and Research LW-324D Pueblo CO 81001	(719) 549-2259	piazza@uscolo.edu
FL	O'Brien, George	Florida International University College of Education DM 283 University Park Campus Miami FL 33199	305-348-2599 F 348-3205	obrieng@servax.fiu.edu
FL	Soon, Yee-Ping	Florida International University College of Education DM 299 University Park Campus Miami FL 33199	305-348-3609 F 348-3205	soon@servax.fiu.edu
GA	Brewton, Cherry	Georgia Southern University Dept. of Early Childhood Educ. L. B. 8083 Statesboro GA 30460-8083	912-681-5983, x5121 F 681-5093	cbrewton@gsaixz.cc. gasou.edu
GA	Cass, Michael	West Georgia College College of Education Department of Special Education Carrollton GA 30118	770-836-4452	mcass@westga.edu

U.S.	NAME	ADDRESS	PHONE & FAX	E-MAIL
HI	Walton, Frank	University of Hawaii College of Education 1776 University Ave Honolulu HI 96822	808-956-9993 F 956-3918	franwal@uhunix.uhcc. hawaii.edu
HI	Zilliox, Joseph	University of Hawaii College of Education 1776 University Ave Honolulu HI 96822	808-956-5358 F 956-3918	zilliox@uhunix.uhcc. hawaii.edu
IA	Voyles, Martha	Grinnell College Department of Education PO Box 805 Grinnell IA 50112	515-269-3053 F 269-4285	voylesm@ac.grin.edu
ID	Kelly, Gwendolyn	University of Idaho College of Education Moscow ID 83844	208-885-6190 F 885-7607	gkelly@raven.csrv. uidaho.edu
ID	Miller, Rickie	Boise State University Elementary Education and Specialized Studies 1910 University Drive Boise ID 83725	208-385-3044	millerr@bsu.idbsu.edu
IN	Breault, Rick	University of Indianapolis Dept. of Teacher Education 1400 East Hanna Ave Indianapolis IN 46227-3697	317-788-3489 F 788-3300	breault@gandlf.uindy.edu
IN	Krockover, Gerald	Purdue University Curriculum & Instruction 1442 LAEB West Lafayette IN 47907-1442	317-494-0491 F 494-7938	xvp2@sage.cc.purdue.edu
IN	Shepardson, Dan	Purdue University Curriculum & Instruction 1442 LAEB West Lafayette IN 47907-1442	317-494-5284 F 494-7938	shepards@vm.cc.purdue. edu
IN	Theobald, Marie	University of Indianapolis Dept. of Teacher Education 1400 East Hanna Ave. Indianapolis IN 46227-3697	317-788-3367 F 788-3300	theobald@gandlf. uindy.edu
KS	Attivo, Barbara	Wichita State University Box 28, College of Education 1845 Fairmount Ave. Wichita KS 67260-0028	316-689-3322 F 689-3302	attivo@wsuhub. uc.twsu.edu
KS	Sherman, Twyla	Wichita State University Box 28, College of Education 1845 Fairmount Ave. Wichita KS 67260-0028	316-689-3322 F 689-3302	sherman@wsuhub. uc.twsu.edu

131

U.S.	NAME	ADDRESS	PHONE & FAX	E-MAIL
KS	Yeotis, Catherine	Wichita State University Box 28, College of Education 1845 Fairmount Ave. Wichita KS 67260-0028	316-689-3322 F 689-3302	yeotis@wsuhub. uc.twsu.edu
KY	Boram, Robert	Morehead State University Department of Physical Sciences Morehead KY 40351	606-783-2931 F 783-5002	r.boram@msuacad. morehead-st.edu
KY	Hines, S. Maxwell	University of Louisville Dept. of Secondary Education 273 School of Ed. Bldg Louisville KY 40292	502-852-0595 F 852-0726	smhine01@ulkyvm. louisville.edu
KY	Karp, Karen	University of Louisville Elementary Education - 243 Louisville KY 40292	502-852-1654 F 852-0726	kskarp01@ulkyvm. louisville.edu
KY	Matthew, Kathleen	Western Kentucky University #1 Big Red Way TPH 322 Bowling Green KY 42101	502-745-6321 F 745-6474	matthkl@wkuvx1. wku.edu
KY	Saxon, Joyce	Morehead State University Dept. of Mathematical Sciences UPO 700 Morehead KY 40351	606-783-2923 F 783-5002	j.saxon@msuacad. morehead-st.edu
KY	Mikovch, Alice	Western Kentucky University #1 Big Red Way TPH 318 Bowling Green KY 42101	502-745-4611 F 745-6474	mikovak@wkuvx1. wku.edu
MI	Freed, Shirley	Andrews University Dept. of Teaching and Learning Bell Hall Room 013B Berrien Springs MI 49104	616-471-6163 616-471-3480 F 471-6374	freed@andrews.edu
MI	Johnson, David	Eastern Michigan University Department of Mathematics Ypsilanti MI 48197	313-487-1290 x1444	mth_johnson@ emuvax.emich.edu
MI	Novak, John	Eastern Michigan University Department of Biology Ypsilanti MI 48197	313-487-2312 F 487-9235	bio_novak@emuvax. emich.edu
MI	Ostrander, Ray	Andrews University Dept. of Teaching and Learning 014E Bell Hall Berrien Springs MI 49104	616-471-6365 F 471-6374	ostrandr@andrews.edu
MO	Lucido, Patricia Ann	Northwest Missouri State University Garrett-Strong 317 800 University Drive Maryville MO 64468-6001	816-562-1605 F 562-1900	plucido@acad. nwmissouri.edu

U.S.	NAME	ADDRESS	PHONE & FAX	E-MAIL
MS	Freeman, Pamela	Mississippi State University Curriculum & Instruction PO Box 6331 Mississippi State, MS 39762	601-325-3747 F 325-8784	pamfree@ra.msstate.edu
MT	Charron, Elisabeth	Montana State University at Bozeman c/o STEP Project 401 Linfield Bozeman MT 59717	406-994-5952 F 994-3733	charron@mathfs. math.montana.edu
MT	Tande, Korinne	Montana State University at Northern Department of Education Box 7751 Havre MT 59501	406-265-3745 F 265-3711	tande@nmc1.nmclites.edu
NC	Levin, Barbara	U. of North Carolina - Greensboro Curriculum & Instruction 345 Curry Building Greensboro NC 27412-5001	910-334-3443 F 334-4120	levinb@dewey.uncg.edu
NC	Matthews, Catherine	U. of North Carolina - Greensboro Curriculum & Instruction 313 Curry Building Greensboro NC 27412-5001	910-334-3444 F 334-4120	matthewb@steffi. uncg.edu
NC	McCoy, Leah	Wake Forest University PO Box 7266 Tribble C101 Winston-Salem NC 27109	910-759-5498 F 759-4591	mccoy@wfu.edu
NJ	Curriero, Frank	Jersey City State College ACI Dept 2039 Kennedy Blvd Jersey City NJ 07305-1597	201-200-2000	
NM	Gee, Donna	Eastern New Mexico University Elementary Education Station 25 Portales NM 88130	505-562-2391 F 562-2523	geed@email.enmu.edu
NY	Bogan, Huey	College of St. Rose School of Education 432 Western Ave. Albany NY 12203	518-454-5270 F 458-5446	boganh@rosnet.strose.edu

U.S.	NAME	ADDRESS	PHONE & FAX	E-MAIL
NY	Gillette, Maureen	College of St. Rose School of Education 432 Western Ave. Albany NY 12203	518-454-5176 F 458-5446	gillettm@rosnet.strose.edu
NY	Peters, Brenda	College of St. Rose School of Education 432 Western Ave. Albany NY 12203	518-458-5460 F 458-5446	petersb@rosnet.strose.edu
NY	Smith-Hobson, Sheila	Lehman College 250 Bedford Park Blvd. W. Carman Hall B-38 Bronx NY 10468-1589	718-960-8175 F 960-8997	sshobson@igc.org
OH	Beeth, Michael	Ohio State University 253 Arps Hall 1945 N. High Street Columbus OH 43210-1172	614-292-5377 F 292-7695	mbeeth@magnus. acs.ohio-state.edu
OH	Grote, Michael	Ohio Wesleyan University Department of Education 214E Phillips Hall Delaware OH 43015	614-368-3561 F 368-3299	mggrote@cc.owu.edu
OK	Hodgden, Aurora	Phillips University Department of Education 100 South University Ave Enid OK 73701	405-237-4433 x 381	
OR	Higgins, Karen	Oregon State University School of Education Education Hall Corvallis OR 97331-3502	503-737-4201 F 737-2040	higginsk@ccmail.orst.edu
OR	Niess, Margaret (Maggie)	Oregon State University Science and Mathematics Educ. Weniger 253 Corvallis OR 97331-3502	503-737-1818 F 737-1817	niessm@ucs.orst.edu
PA	Lord, Thomas	Indiana University of Penn. Biology-S Education Weyandt Hall Indiana PA 15705	412-357-2484 F 357-5700	trlord@grove.iup.edu
PA	Stempien, Margaret	Indiana University of Penn. Department of Mathematics Stright Hall Indiana PA 15705	412-357-3793 F 357-5700	mmstemp@grove.iup.edu
PA	Twiest, Meghan	Indiana University of Penn. Elementary & Early Childhood Education 313 Davis Hall Indiana PA 15705	412-357-2404 F 357-7515	mmtwiest@grove.iup.edu

U.S.	NAME	ADDRESS	PHONE & FAX	E-MAIL
SD	Spethmann, Dorothy	Dakota State University School of Education East Hall Madison SD 57042	605-256-5160 F 256-5316	spethmad@columbia. dsu.edu
VT	Erb, Clinton	University of Vermont Dept. of Education 535 Waterman Building Burlington VT 05405	802-656-3356 F 656-0004	c_erb@uvmvax.uvm.edu
VT	Kenny, Mary Josephine (Jody)	St. Michael's College Dept. of Undergraduate Education Box 234 Colchester VT 05439	802-654-2376 F 655-3680	j_kenny@smcvax. smcvt.edu
VT	Morris, Joyce	University of Vermont P.E.C.D. 539 Waterman Building Burlington VT 05405	802-656-3356 F 656-0004	jmorris@moose.uvm.edu
VT	Rathbone, Charles	University of Vermont 534b Waterman Building CESS:UVM Burlington VT 05405	802-656-3356 F 656-0004	crathbon@moose.uvm.edu
WI	Brooks, Patsy	Alverno College PO Box 343922 Milwaukee WI 53234-3922	414-382-6196 F 382-6354	pbrooks@omnifest. uwm.edu
WI	Madison, Sandra	U. of Wisconsin - Stevens Point Dept of Mathematics & Computing Stevens Point WI 54481	715-346-4612 F346-2561	smadison@uwspmail. uwsp.edu
WI	Welty, Kenneth	University of Wisconsin-Stout Communication, Education & Training Menomonie WI 54751	715-232-1206 F 232-1441	weltyk@uwstout.edu
WV	Werner, Judy	West Virginia University Curriculum & Instruction PO Box 6122 Morgantown WV 26506-6122	304-293-3442 x 1314 F 293-3802	jaw@wvnvm.wvnet.edu